6/01

GOD

in the

MOVIES

GOD
in the
MOVIES

Albert J. Bergesen

Andrew M. Greeley

with a preface by Roger Ebert

Transaction Publishers
New Brunswick (U.S.A.) and London (U.K.)

Library of Congress Catalog Number: 00-034406
ISBN: 0-7658-0020-9
Printed in the United States of America

Library of Congress Cataloging-in-Publication Data

Bergesen, Albert J.
    God in the movies / Albert J. Bergesen, Andrew M. Greeley ; with
a preface by Roger Ebert.
    p. cm.
Includes bibliographical references and index.
ISBN 0-7658-0020-9 (alk. paper)
1. Motion pictures— Religious aspects. I. Greeley, Andrew M., 1928-
II. Greeley, Andrew M. III. Title.

PN1995.5 .B44 2000
791.43'68231—dc21   00-034406

Contents

Preface

Roger Ebert

The authors of this book are quite right that most people are blind to the religious symbolism in the movies they see. They do not look for God when they go to the movies, although it would be odd indeed if She (as Andrew Greeley often refers to Him) was not reflected in the dominant art form of the twentieth century. Recently I have been engaged in a running battle with those who feel Martin Scorsese's *Bringing Out the Dead* is one of his lesser films—even a failure. I believe it belongs with the best of his work. What has amazed me in my discussions is that no one ever refers to the spiritual content of the film, and yet it is specifically Christian from beginning to end, and not just because its action incorporates the cardinal acts of mercy and all of the seven deadly sins, takes place over three days and has a Christ-figure for its hero. It is Christian because it considers with the question of what a good man can accomplish in a world that seems to be the devil's playground. (It is not a coincidence that the action all takes place in Hell's Kitchen.)

The film was written for Scorsese by Paul Schrader, the author of all his most specifically religious work (*Taxi Driver, Raging Bull, The Last Temptation of Christ*). Schrader is a Calvinist by birth and upbringing, a man occasionally overtaken by clouds of gloom and the conviction that he has made his last film, that there is no longer room for his work in today's crass commercial climate. One day a few years ago, as we sat in the shade of some California trees, he said that he and Scorsese were existentialists in an age of irony. "I'm really of the existential tradition, the twentieth century tradition," he said. "Tarantino is tying into the ironic hero. I know the existential hero's in trouble and I know this century is almost over. But I don't know how nourishing the ironic hero can be....The existential dilemma is, 'should I live?' And the ironic answer is, 'does it matter?' Everything in the ironic world has quotation marks around it. You don't actually kill somebody; you 'kill' them. It doesn't really matter if you put the baby in front of the runaway car because it's only a 'baby' and it's only a 'car.'"

The film he was working on just then was *Touch*, an adaptation of an Elmore Leonard story about a stigmatic, a former Franciscan, who can help people by touching them. I honor Schrader's impulse in making it. It basically asks: What do you do when your religion calls your bluff and turns out to be real, and you can't get away with safe, middle-class piety any more, but are called to behave like those fanatics in the Lives of the Saints? How then should you behave in the real world? A woman in the hero's life offers to do his laundry, and then pauses, and wonders if it's all right to put stigmatic blood through the wash.

The films considered by Andrew Greeley and Albert Bergesen in this book all put the blood through the wash, in one way or another. They dare to consider the divine in the context of the carnal—not only in their stories, but in their very form, which is the Hollywood entertainment film. Most people, as the authors observe, do not consider these movies from a religious point of view. Even when a character is clearly considered to be God, as Audrey Hepburn is in *Always*, most audiences, I imagine, think of her not as God but as "God," a character in a movie. Or as an angel, which was my impulse. One of the most awesomely spiritual films I have ever seen is Lars von Trier's *Breaking the Waves*, in which, as Greeley observes, the dour Scottish church elders remove the bells from their church tower as too festive, and get their comeuppance when the peals of celestial bells ring out from the very heavens. The impact of this film was so powerful that when it premiered at the Cannes Film Festival, one of the American critics, from a very secular New York weekly, fled to the ladies' room in tears. Janet Maslin of the *New York Times* went in to comfort her, and both were locked inside the Palais des Festivals. Yet when the film went on to win prizes at Cannes and Academy Award recognition, most of the reviews described the frankness of its sex, not the frankness of its spirituality. It was as specifically and obviously and deliberately spiritual as any film I can think of, but it was not discussed in those terms.

Maybe we are embarrassed to discuss religion and the movies at the same time. Perhaps when we have spiritual experiences we translate them into mundane terms as quickly as we can. I know that I have been shaken to the depth of my existence by a few movies (*Do the Right Thing*, *Cries and Whispers*, and *Ikiru* for example), and I also know that even broadly popular films like *Ghost*, *Field of Dreams*, and *The Sixth Sense* got people worked up. The studios can never understand it when a film like *The Sixth Sense*, which is mostly downbeat, contemplative, and deliberately confusing, attracts enormous audiences and repeat business. It is because it gives people something to talk about and think about, and they appreciate it. One of the values of this book is that it considers the ways in which those films may have touched many of the members of their audiences—whether they were prepared to admit it or not.

Andrew Greeley and I have conducted a long-running discussion about God and the movies over the years. Not long ago we were sitting late in a Middle Eastern restaurant near the Michigan shore, lamenting the inaccuracies of so many of the movies about angels. (Whenever an angel appears in a movie and starts talking about how long he's been waiting for a pizza, I want to take him aside and break the news that as an angel he is *not* a reincarnated human as Hollywood seems determined to believe, but a spiritual being who never has and never will possess the equipment to eat a pizza. *Wings of Desire* has it right—you have to turn in your wings, and along with the pizza you have to accept such human indignities as disease and death.)

Greeley told me about his university courses on God in the movies, and indeed I think the course had its inspiration in his thoughts after seeing *Jacob's Ladder* (his thoughts on the subject in general I gather followed from *All That Jazz*). What is so valuable about his courses, and about this book he has written with Bergesen, is that it reminds readers and students that *movies really are about something*. They really are. They are not simply devices to distract us for two hours, although that's all a lot of audience members get out of them. They embody our dreams, desires, and aspirations, and give form to them. And if God takes the form of Audrey Hepburn—well, why not? If we were made in Her image and likeness, then which of us does not look like God? And imagining myself saying that to Greeley, I imagine his answer: "Yes, and Audrey Hepburn more than most!"

Introduction

We are writing about religion and popular culture from the perspective of sociology. One of us is a sociologist of religion who is interested in (perhaps obsessed by) popular culture. The other of us is a sociologist of popular culture who is interested in (and perhaps obsessed by, though arguably less so) religion. We both believe that there is something to be learned about American society by studying its popular culture. Those who produce popular culture depend for their livelihood on their judgments about what interests their audiences. Therefore, when they, very gingerly, turn to religion for the subject matter of their work, they tell us something about what they think American religion is.

Such a perspective tells us both less and more than survey data about American religion, less because the popular culture approach to religion hardly reflects a random sample of American beliefs and values, more because popular culture presents a much richer and more emotionally resonant portrait than do statistical tables. We are both impressed, however, by the basic similarities in the findings of the two different research enterprises, although the God in the movies is, if anything, more gracious than the God of the surveys. Indeed we believe that, with a single exception, the God in the movies is closer to the image of God in the Jewish and Christian heritages than the God of the surveys. The God of the movies is the God Americans might like to believe in though not the God many Americans feel they have to believe in.

We choose the movies for our investigation because we are both incorrigible movie addicts and because it seems to us that the movies are the most vivid of all the lively arts—and probably the one best suited to the God question. We chose the movies we did for this study because they seem to us to be the best suited for our project—which means that they are the ones we like the most.

We are not theologians (for which we might say *Deo Gratias*!). We will try as sociologists to reflect on the meaning of the images of God as pre-

1

sented in the movies but we explicitly reject the notion that we are offering, to be redundant, a theology of God. It is our impression that most theologians these days are more interested in politics than in God, anyway.

Both of us do, however, believe in God, a belief for which we do not apologize, one of us in a Protestant God and the other of us in a Catholic God. As we work together, we find that the two Gods are very like one another, a fact which we find ecumenically reassuring. With some reservations we like the God in the movies and rather hope that He/She approves of our work.

We also believe that any God claiming to be radically different from the God of the Movies (with the exception of a single film) is an imposter and ought not to be believed in.

We chose to write this book for ordinary people rather than just for our sociological colleagues, though we freely grant them permission to read it. Just as popular culture is designed for the populace, we believe that analysis of popular culture should appeal to the populace. Somehow, we believe it is unfair (perhaps even sacrilegious) to write about God in popular culture only for those who are capable of reading the journals of our profession.

We are, be it noted, not prepared to apologize to anyone for being either sociologists or theists. We are not attempting, God forbid, to make converts to our theism. We do suggest, quite meekly, that the God of the Movies is a God worth believing in. If there should be a God (and sociology as such can't know whether there is) and if the real God should be like the God of Movies, then that is a very good news indeed.

Sometimes God in the Movies is portrayed by a human actor. Sometimes God is present merely as a force or an energy, often by light or as a lacy white cloud as in *Truly, Madly, Deeply.* Sometimes God lurks just beneath the story as in *Flatliners* or *The Rapture* or *Breaking the Waves.* Three of our films were not made in America but they are consistent with the depiction of God in the other films.

Some will think that it is blasphemous to seek God in the Movies. God is beyond human utterance. To see humans as representatives of God is idolatry. We do not agree. Since we are humans, we are forced to imagine God in human terms, as imperfect as we know these terms to be. To exclude metaphors (sacraments) is to preclude the possibility of saying anything about God.

Some academics will think that it is traitorous to pretend that there is a God. We do not agree with them either. There may not be a God but then, on the other hand, there may. Either assumption has its problems. The latter is faced with the problem that there is evil. The former with the problem that there is anything at all. We do not argue that there is a God. We note rather that for most of human history and indeed even today the pertinent questions is not whether there is a God but what God is like. It is to the latter question we address ourselves. Sociologists cannot say that God *is*, but they can analyze various answers to the question of what God might be like.

Our book has its origins in a course Andrew Greeley compiled on God in the Movies and taught at both the University of Chicago and the University of Arizona. He undertook the course because of his research on religious symbols and the impact on him and because of the movie *All That Jazz* which he describes in chapter 4. Albert Bergesen taught the course with him at the University of Arizona and then subsequently taught it by himself during a summer session. We are grateful to the students in these courses for their challenges, suggestions, and insights. The next two chapters will outline our individual reactions to the project. Then we will begin to analyze each of the films which we think attempt to tell us something about God.

Albert Bergesen wrote chapters 2, 6, 7, 8, 11, 13, and 15. Andrew Greeley wrote chapters 1, 3, 4, 5, 9, 10, 12, and 14 and the conclusion as well as this introduction. Both authors, however, commented extensively and with considerable effect on the chapters written by the other.

We dedicate this book to our colleagues at the University of Arizona for putting up with us (sometimes perhaps heroically) and to Susie.

1

God in the Movies

Let's suppose that you're God.

Let's also suppose that You're pretty much the reality that You have described in the various Scriptures, indeed that You are, as You have said, Love—merciful love, passionate love, forgiving love, love which is the end of that wisdom of which fear is only the beginning. Let us further suppose that You yearn, as You claim, for a loving response from Your people, a response which one might call loving faith and faithful love. Finally let us suppose that You are determined to pursue Your people with all the skillful implacability that You possess.

Then what?

The sociologist who studies religious images and stories cannot, as such, say whether there is a God or whether, should God be, He lives up to the claims He is alleged to make in the Holy Books. But a sociologist can speculate about what such a God might do as one part of Her strategy.

Let us make one more supposition: let us suppose that, since as God You are everywhere, You are also present for the homilies and sermons which Your people hear every weekend. You would have difficulty in recognizing Yourself in most of these orations. BORING, you would agree with the teens. If Your folk do not find the God of the homilies as attractive, as appealing, as irresistible as You claim to be, then You might turn to Hollywood. Perhaps, You think, a God of the Movies might reveal more of Your overwhelming beauty, Your implacable mercy, and Your dazzling goodness than the weekend sermons disclose.

God conspiring with filmmakers to short circuit the homilies? Surely that is an outrageous conceit, isn't it? It is, however, a model which I hope to show fits the data.

Why do filmmakers introduce God into their stories? Each filmmaker will have his or her own particular reason but at a more general level, the "God story" is a story about the mystery of life and death. Tell me who your God is or what He is like and I'll know immediately what you believe about the mystery of life and death. All the God films in one way or another deal directly and explicitly with this mystery, sometimes with remarkable (if implicit and perhaps pre-conscious) metaphorical sophistication.

"If God were really like that," a teenage woman remarked to her companion as they walked out of *Oh, God* ahead of me. "So sympathetic, so loving, so kind, I could really have faith in Him."

Her friend was surprised. "But she is!" she said.

Ah, but that's the problem isn't it?

"God is like Audrey Hepburn in *Always?*" an agnostic colleague exclaimed when I propounded my theory. "If She really were like that, I'd believe in God again."

"God more sexy that Jessica Lange in *All That Jazz*?" a fellow priest raised his eyebrows. "Yeah, well, maybe you're right. Except She had better be even more sexy!"

See what I mean? Doesn't it kind of smell like a plot?

A man is about to die in a hospital bed. We cut to a dark and shabby office where he has been sitting in judgment on his life with a beautiful woman in bridal white. The woman removes her hat and veil. We see him again on the hospital bed, on the edge of expiration. Then we return to the dusty office where his life has been reviewed. The woman's shoulders are bare, she has discarded her bridal dress and lets down her hair; she is still wearing a white undergarment and smiles in anticipation and invitation; a rose is attached to her wrist as she takes his hand. Back in the hospital room he seems to have stopped breathing. Then the woman appears again, clearly naked though we see only her shoulders. She seems vulnerable, eager, and very much in love.

The scene is from the late Bob Fosse's 1979 musical *All That Jazz*, a Cannes Festival Golden Palm winner. Joe Gideon (Roy Scheider) escapes death in this interlude and does not make love this time with the Angel of Death— Angelique (Jessica Lange) she is called in the credits. The consummation of their love affair must wait to the end of the film. The scene is so quick and so deftly edited that one can watch *All That Jazz* many times without catching its implications and without realizing fully that Fosse is suggesting that the Angel may be, indeed probably is, God.

Earlier in the film Joe Gideon (a Fosse alter ego), engaged in what might be called in Catholic terms his "particular judgment," flips through his file of reviews and complains that he has done nothing worthwhile in his life. Angelique—who is consistently more positive about him than he is about himself—replies that his reviews show what a great success he has been. But, he argues, he has never made anything perfect like a rose. Angelique is amused; only God can make a rose. Gideon says that he feels like congratulating God every time he sees a rose. She laughs and says that's one of the greatest con lines ever, apparently accepting it as a compliment to herself. Then the film cuts to Cliff Gorman as the stand-up comedian who is doing a routine about Elizabeth Kübler-Ross's stages of dying. Almost at once we return to Angelique who is holding a rose. The comic bellows, "Oh, God!" and we see once more the beautiful, confident, and ever so slightly scary face of Angelique.

God is often portrayed as an aroused lover, hungering for his people and sometimes as a woman. In Exodus: 20, at the beginning of the decalogue, the Holy One proclaims that he is a "passionate" or "jealous" God. I am told by those familiar with the Hebrew of the TNK that the word is used elsewhere to describe an aroused groom "breathing after" his bride. In Hosea, God is represented as a husband desperately desiring his faithless wife. In Deuteronomy: 32 God presents Herself as a mother giving birth to and nursing her child. In commentary on the Song of Songs (if not in the actual intent of the author), the ravenous groom is compared to God. In the Christian Easter Liturgy, the candle is plunged into the water with the prayer (in Latin before the translation was bowdlerized) that the candle might impregnate the waters. In Isaiah God compares himself to the bride of Israel's youth, a woman giving birth (42) and a mother who will not forget her children. Fosse, however, is the first non-biblical artist of whom I am aware in the Jewish and Christian traditions to use the metaphor of an aroused woman to hint at God's love. There are two endings to the film: in the first Joe Gideon strides down the long tunnel of the near-death experience (which now has become a common metaphor in films such as *Fearless*) towards his glowing fair bride. In the second a plastic body bag is zipped up in the hospital morgue—either the cold slab or the passionate warmth of the wedding bed.

All God talk is metaphorical. All metaphors say that something is like something else and yet not like it. Juliet is like the sun and yet not like the sun. Creative Beauty (should It in fact exist) is reflected by created beauty. Are attractive and loving members of the opposite sex metaphors for God? Is their naked beauty, properly cherished and respected, a clue to God's beauty?

Why not?

Is sexual attraction a metaphor for the relationship between God and his people?

St. Paul thought so.

My students sometimes protest that Joe Gideon lusts for Angelique. But lust means the desire to use and to exploit, which Gideon would never dare. All right, they say, but Angelique desires him. God doesn't desire us. Yeah? Go back and read the Hebrew scriptures.

Another woman played God in Stephen Spielberg's *Always* (1989), a remake of a 1943 film *A Guy Named Joe* (featuring Spencer Tracy, Irene Dunne and Van Johnson). It is perhaps the worst film ever made about God but with (for this sociologist) one of the more wondrous images of God—Audrey Hepburn. The hotshot fire-fighter pilot Pete, (Richard Dreyfuss) is killed and his companion Dorinda (Holly Hunter) finds a new lover (Brad Johnson). But Pete refuses to accept his death and keeps coming back from the dead to interfere with the new relationship, although a being-in-white with whom he is in dialogue in another world begs him not to do so. Rather she says, with infinite gentleness and affection, he should give up the past and go on to what is yet to come.

The woman finally wins his surrender. His wife has her new love and he goes on to whatever is next. Audrey Hepburn is an appealing metaphor for the womanly love of God, a God who cares deeply, patiently, tenderly, and with that gentle amusement which women usually display towards the other and childlike sex of the species.

Some of my students, uneasy about God as a beautiful woman, have argued that Ms. Lange and Ms. Hepburn were only angels (though to a person they say that they hope God is like Ms. Hepburn). But they are trying to dodge the challenge of metaphor. In the Jewish Scriptures the Angel of the Lord (Malek Yahweh) is in fact the Lord in human form. In the Christian scriptures, the angel is a direct and immediate reflection of God.

In two other films of the turn of the decade between the eighties and the nineties, God appears in male form.

Mr. Destiny is an unsuccessful 1991 revision of *It's a Wonderful Life.* It has, however, a marvelous conceit: God, no mere and bumbling angel this time, is played by the smooth, suave Michael Caine. Larry Burrows (Jim Belushi) is a young man who struck out in the last of the ninth with the bases loaded at the age of fifteen and who blames all the subsequent troubles of his life on that failure. He encounters Caine, wearing sleeve garters and a vest, in a mysterious bar and unloads his troubles. Does he want to live his life over? You bet he does. He drinks a fizzing, smoking concoction which will change his life into what it would have been if he had not done a Casey at the Bat. Caine accompanies him, first in a cab and later in a limousine, wearing a cab driver's cap (as Burns does). What are you, Belushi demands, an angel or something?

Not exactly, Caine responds. Let's say that I am the one—and he pokes his fingers in the air in the form of a circle, touching off little sparks of light—who arranges the choices for you to make. He thus solves in a single reply, the whole problem of grace and freedom. Naturally the experiment doesn't work and naturally Larry is very happy to return to his old life. At the end, however, we are back in the ballpark where he whiffed and he is fifteen once again. It is night and the kid sits in the grandstand of the empty stadium. Caine appears behind. It's all right, he says. Everything will be all right. Just trust me. The sixteen-year-old stomps away, muttering, "a lot that old geezer knows!"

The audience laughs because they know who the "old geezer" is.

Jacob's Ladder (1991) written by Bruce Joel Rubin and directed by Adrian Lyne, is the story of a Vietnam veteran, Jacob Singer (Tim Robbins), who was poisoned by experimental drugs designed to turn him into a killing machine—and may have died in Vietnam. Now he is pursued by government agents who want to eliminate all traces of their experiments. His only confidant is his chiropractor—Danny Aiello. Danny Aiello as God? Jacob in the scripture wrestled with the Lord did he not? So Jacob wrestles with the chiropractor.

Jacob says to Louis (Aiello), "You, know you look like an angel, Louis, an overgrown cherub . . . you're a life-saver." Louis agrees that he is. Later Jacob tells Louis that he doesn't want to die. Louis says he'll see what he can do about it.

The government agents capture him and drag him off to a hellish hospital where he is turned over to a team of demonic doctors who poke tubes into his veins and probe at him with instruments of torture. The chiropractor learns of his friend's fate, rushes to the hospital, routs the demons, pulls the tubes out of Jacob's arms and legs, knocks over the medical machines, and drags Jacob out of hell. As he heals Jacob's injuries, he quotes Eckart's argument that hell is the part of your life you won't let go of.

At the end, Jacob who perhaps this time has really died, appears at the entrance of his apartment building. Go right on in, Doctor Singer, the doorman says, your wife has already gone upstairs. He enters a luxurious apartment and, led by a son who was thought to be dead, ascends a stairway (a ladder like that the biblical Jacob saw ascending to heaven) bathed in light up to the second floor. Both Caine and Aiello are God figures who beseech, lure, beg their charges to let go so they might go on.

In Joel Schumacher's remarkable 1990 film *Flatliners*, God appears only as the light in the classic Near Death Experience imagery. A group of medical students Julia Roberts, Kevin Bacon, Kiefer Sutherland, William Baldwin, and Oliver Platt) determine to induce death in one another and report back when they are revived (if they are revived) on the nature of the experience. They do not find the figure of light at the end of the tunnel because they never get that far in their journeys. Rather they go through the judgment process and discover that they must atone for the hidden crimes of their lives. Some of their victims are still alive and some are dead. The students begin to be haunted in their lives outside of the hospital and realize, all too slowly, that they must do penance for their offenses or they will lose their sanity and their lives.

The case of Rachel (Ms. Roberts) is a bit different. Her challenge is not to seek forgiveness but to grant it. Her father was a regular army non-com who had become a drug addict and had blown out his brains in her presence. He is trapped in a Purgatory-like situation in which he must remain until she is ready to forgive him (which she has not done). When she discovers his plight, she promptly and graciously forgives him and he is freed and absorbed by light.

At the end of the film, Nelson (Mr. Sutherland), in a long near-death interlude, finally finds forgiveness from the boy he had killed when he was a child, is bathed in the healing light, and returns a different man than the arrogant person he had been.

Schumacher's religious imagery consists of skilled manipulation of light (white, red, and black and different for each character and blue and yellow for different situations) and darkness. Because of the light the possibility of forgiveness and being forgiven is not terminated by death. If the light is not God, a loving, generous, alluring God, then what is it? (Anthony Minghella in his *Truly, Madly, Deeply* depicts the deity as a fragile but brilliant white cloud floating across a lovely blue sky).

In all five of these films, the characters with whom He has become involved are in "purgatorial" situations, caught between life and death —Roy Scheider, Richard Dreyfuss, Tim Robbins and the young medical students explicitly, Jim Belushi implicitly. They are judging their own lives and simultaneously being judged. In each case the God character is willing to be more generous and forgiving to them than they are to themselves and at the same time pleads with them to give up what they have left behind so that they might go on to something better.

Moreover Jessica Lange, Audrey Hepburn, Michael Caine, Danny Aiello and the comforting white light which lurks beyond the darkness (in *Flatliners*) are all charmers, each in their own way. The Ground of Being is portrayed as loving, patient, determined, and passionate, a God who has fallen in love with His creatures and will stop at nothing to win their love in return; an improvising God who never gives up on His creatures no matter how much they have given up on themselves; a seductive God who calls humans out of themselves and begs them to leave the past behind (even when the past is life itself)and to risk the future; an ingenious God who says that forgiveness is always possible, a God of second chances, a God who beckons to us with powerful light and passionate love.

As I say, this consistent image of God in very different films by very different filmmakers, is just too suspicious to be an accident. Someone is up to something.

A God who calls, who beckons, who attracts, who invites, who seduces; such metaphors may not reveal the meaning of life at all, but if they do, then that is irresistibly good news. Perhaps one would still not want to believe in such a God. Or could not. Perhaps one would demand, as Job did, explanations. Yet, as my teenage friend said, if God were really like that . . .

So is the passion of Jessica Lange in *All That Jazz* an appropriate metaphor? Surely it is, so long as we realize that God, should there be

one, claims in the scriptures to be more beautiful than the most beautiful of humans and more passionately in love with us than any human
lover could be. Ms. Lange, vulnerable, naked, deeply in love, is inadequate as a metaphor by defect rather than by excess: God is even more
passionately in love with humans.

God vulnerable? What else would a God be who is involved in a love
relationship, as the Holy Books contend, with humankind? I suspect
that, as the homiletic boredom continues to dominate, such a God might
become even more outrageous in his conspiracy with the filmmakers to
essay an answer to Job's complaint.

Thus in Lars Von Trier's Cannes prize-winning film *Breaking the
Waves*, a dour and grim group of men (no women permitted) are apparently burying a young woman named Bess (Emily Watson) on a deso-
late island off the coast of Scotland. The elders from her stern Calvinist
church, so stern it has removed the bells from its bell tower, condemn
her to hell for all eternity. In the meantime, her husband, for whose
restoration to health she has sacrificed her virtue and her life, has stolen
her body from the casket to bury her with honor at sea from the deck of
the oil rig on which he works. Shortly after he bids her a sad farewell,
he is awakened by other members of the crew. Bells are pealing over
the rig and the North Sea and the island. God is vindicating the young
woman, confirming his conversations with her (which as the film goes
on have become warmer and more loving) and canceling the judgment
of the elders of her wee kirk. The conversations he had with Bess (God
speaking to her in her own voice) were real. God is not a stern, self-
righteous church elder. In the pealing bells God confirms that his love
is stronger than his justice, his mercy stronger than his anger. Or as film
critic Roger Ebert put it, God not only knows everything but understands much more than we give him credit for.

Ms. Watson was nominated for an Academy Award as best actress
that year, an unusual event since, as one critic has remarked, her portrait of a saint may be the best since Marie Falconetti played Joan of
Arc in Carl Theodor Dreyer's famous silent film.

In *Commandments*, God seems to have manipulated the filmmaker
into responding directly to all the Jobs of human history. A small crowd
gathers around a beached whale near Montauk (which I am told is on a
place called Long Island). A brave person slices open the belly of the
whale, water and fish flow out, and then the body of a man. The man,
Seth Warner (Aidan Quinn), revives and stares at the sun and the blue

sky in grateful astonishment. He has been waging war with God. His wife has drowned, a tornado has destroyed his house (the only one on its street to be so afflicted), he has lost his job, lightning struck him (and his dog). God has violated the Covenant. For revenge Seth has violated all the commandments, including "thou shalt not kill," the last by throwing himself off a lighthouse during a hurricane. God trumps the complaints of a modern Job with the Sign of Jonah. Even when a man abandons God, God does not abandon him. Seth Warner demands an answer, God gives him one: Jonah trumps Job!

Breaking the Waves and *Commandments* certainly push the envelope, just as *All That Jazz* did, the latter towards a God who seduces, the former towards a God who, how shall we say it, does not mess around when He wants to demonstrate the power of His love. Can this development be merely an accident or is it not the sign of a very sophisticated plotter?

Is this conspiracy theory of mine a demented fantasy? A dementia caused by reading too many BORING theology books? A faith that has finally gone over the top? Do I really expect readers to believe in the kind of God one encounters in the movies?

Not really. I ask only for the concession that a God like that would be one worth believing in, no matter how many explanations might be required of Him.

Moreover, if the God of the Holy Books is really what the books claim, then She would stop at nothing to disclose Her beauty and Her love to us. Why not disclose Herself through the movies?

If that be the case, then the News is very Good indeed.

A.M.G.

2

Movies as Story and Metaphor

Our premise is that religion is story before it is anything else and after it is everything else, as hope-renewing experiences are captured in symbols and woven into stories that are told and retold. Like other social activities, storytelling occurs throughout society. In families we tell children stories; in schools teachers tell students; at work and play we tell each other, and in church and synagogue stories are told as part of the worship service. To this list we wish to add the movies. To say the movies tell stories is a bit obvious. But the visual representation of God on the big screen is not expected given Hollywood's purported hostility to religion.

When we say God in the movies exactly what do we mean? We don't mean movies that are formally about religion, like *Ben Hur* or *The Last Temptation of Christ*. Nor movies about people's religious beliefs or how they are tested and pull them through rough times, although that may be a context within which God makes an appearance on screen. Nor, finally, are we talking about Woody Allen-like movies that have philosophical discussions over the existence and meaning of God, as in his *Crimes and Misdemeanors*. The movies we are thinking about are not so much formally religious, as ordinary mass release Hollywood type movies. What distinguishes them the most is that God makes an appearance on screen. What we have discovered is that, contrary to the popular belief that today's movies are Godless and indifferent to religion, there is not only a surprising number of references to religion and faith, but actual efforts at visually representing God on the big screen. God is in the movies more than we think. On the surface this seems odd because movies are more concerned with entertainment than religion.

Movies are entertainment, of course, but this is our very point that religion arises from hope-renewing experiences that are put in entertaining stories and are shared to elicit similar experiences in others. All forms of storytelling are potential avenues for religious expression, of course. We just want to point out the surprising degree to which movies express the religious imagination.

When we examine other societies we seem to have no difficulty decoding the images, symbols, and analogies they use to speak of God. There is no rite so simple or obscure that modern cultural studies hasn't deconstructed to extract the inner religious meaning. But when it comes to contemporary society there seems to be a loss of anthropological nerve. We become traditionalists, and movies by and large are simply not the place we regularly look for expressions of religious sentiment. But if religion is born of hope-renewing experiences and shared in story, then the movies are absolutely a modern outlet for what appears to be the irrepressible human urge to tell stories about the meaning of life.

Listening to such stories is not new. People have always assembled to share their experiences in story. From gathering around the flickering light of open fires to gathering around the projection light on the movie screen, humans assemble in communal solidarity to listen to stories about the beginning and end of life and what it might all mean. The underlying hopes and fears that make up these stories probably haven't changed all that much over time, but what has is the medium in which they are told. Stories told on the stained glass windows of medieval cathedrals held people's attention as they do today on the silver screen. The cineplex is not a religious assembly hall, of course, but it certainly feels similar when the lights go down and the movie begins. There is a quiet stillness, an almost religious seriousness as individuals seem to let go and lose themselves in what unfolds in front of them. It is in these moments, communally gathered, focused upon the unfolding story, that the religious imagination appears, with a surprising number of metaphors for God, in virtually as many shapes and forms as we can imagine.

Many art forms are pressed into service for this social task of storytelling, including short stories, magazine articles, television, poetry, novels, and movies. Our concern here, though, is with stories that everyone knows and talks about, that is, stories that hold people's attention and seem to matter. Over time different forms of expression have been more actively pressed into service for the central task of telling collective stories than others. Movies are only a twentieth-century invention and the novel only rose to prominence in the eighteenth century. Before this, drama and poetry were probably more prominent. But today of all the plays performed on stage, poems recited, and novels read, it seems the movies are the preeminent art form employed in basic, society-wide, perhaps worldwide, storytelling. As Gore Vidal observed, "today, where literature was movies are...art is now sight and sound...movies are the lingua franca of the twentieth century."[1] It's not just that movies are watched more but that they are the art form that generates the most social excitement and passion. When was the last time anyone remembers a heated discussion in the office about a recent poem or novel? It's hard to think of one; but we are always saying, "what did you think of this new movie," but almost never, "did you read this new novel." Even novels like *The Godfather* or popular books by John Grisham or Tom Clancy do not seem to be pressed into service for societal self-reflection until they appear as movies. Television is storytelling too, of course, and we would certainly want to see what was on TV. But because of screen size and average program length TV seems to work better for live events, sports, news, and light entertainment, like the rapid-fire humor of sitcoms. Movies, conversely, provide not only a bigger canvas but allow more time for a story to develop.

Movies, then, are one of the most important media through which underlying social and religious beliefs are expressed. The Western has been linked to American ideologies of individualism and a personal resolution of social problems. In the classic shootout one lives (embodying the good) and one dies (embodying the bad) and the plot has its simple resolution. Along with such political ideologies, gender relations have also been identified as feminist scholarship notes male aggression, power relations, and the subordination of women not only in the Western but in the patriarchal imagination in general. Movies, then, continue to be read to understand basic beliefs about gender, race, age, and, with science fiction, beliefs about the future from the danger of alien invasions, in *The War of the Worlds* or the *Invasion of the Body Snatchers* to the more peaceful vision in *E.T.* While the interpretation of any particular movie may be debatable, no one doubts film reflects basic beliefs, including, we want to argue, beliefs about the nature of God.

That images of God should regularly appear in movies is not an accident. Movies are actually well suited for popular religious expression. In part, this is because they are a general art form whose appeal crosses almost all social divisions. Not since the Shakespearean stage, it has been argued, has the audience of an art form been so general and crossed so many class and education divisions as the movies. While audiences for other art forms (symphony, ballet, modern dance, opera, etc.) are often more specialized the movies don't seem to assume any particular level of knowledge from their audience, providing a genuine mass appeal. There are emphases, of course. Men may attend more action movies, women find personal stories more attractive, and the very young are more often taken to G-rated movies. The market for movies has also continually widened, such that the same movie today is very often seen around the world. This creates the lowest common denominator principle, the idea that the wider the appeal of the movie the less one can assume about level of education, religious persuasion, or sophistication of the audience. Movies, then, are subject to the critique of mass culture: in their effort to find subject matter of interest regardless of education or income content must be dumbed down to lowest common denominator, like gratuitous sex or violence. The growth of blockbuster action films that seem to absorb the energy of major studios is no doubt tied to this continued widening of the world movie audience. To attract audiences around the world what is needed is not only a recognizable star but also a narrative line that is moved along by thrills, spills, colors, and sounds in a virtual nonstop 120-minute cinematic amusement park ride.

But this idea of the lowest common denominator of human experience suggests something else, namely that movies universally touch people regardless of their income, education, or other social affiliations. While movie themes may be base, they are also basic, as fundamental questions about existence. Life and death are one of the, if not the, most common of denominators of humanity, and movies dealing with this topic are well suited to deal with our most basic concerns. To find something common in our existence this way is to raise those big questions so often the subject matter of religion. It is interesting, then, how a common denominator can be at once so crude and base and yet so fundamental and basic. There is, for instance, no experience more universal than the knowledge that we will die, and most importantly for our theory of religion, the hope that such death is somehow not the end. When we encounter experiences that renew hope and immortalize them in story, these acts of popular religion are truly one of the common denominators of all human existence. Such stories, told in different places at different times, constitute the substratum of organized religion. The sociological fact that we are born into already-existing religious traditions means these hope-renewing experiences are most often talked about in the language of preexisting stories. That is, we see the world in terms of our religious backgrounds. This seems inescapable. We rarely see things in completely new ways. But it is also true that we don't entirely retell stories the same way either. New elements are constantly being added reflecting the storteller's time and place. This certainly goes for storytelling where God makes an appearance on the big screen.

For example, in the literature on near-death experiences people seem to regularly report seeing themselves going through a tunnel toward a bright light at the other end. What this means, or why it is so commonly reported is not clear, but such a bright light at the end of a tunnel has often been pressed into service as a cinematic analogy, or metaphor, for God and heaven.

An example of this can be seen in the movie *Fearless,* staring Jeff Bridges. To begin with this is not a particularly religious movie. It is more about personal reactions to traumatic experiences. In this case, Jeff Bridges has survived a plane crash and, in a state of shock and denial of his crash experience, he feels "fearless" and focuses upon helping another survivor get over her trauma. He is successful at this and eventually returns to normal himself. In the movie, though, while choking on a strawberry, Bridges falls unconscious on the dining room floor with his wife desperately trying to revive him. While he lays on the floor with a dazed look, there is a flashback to the airplane crash he lived through. There we see the smoke-filled crashed fuselage, dark and grey, broken in half with the open end flooded by a bright light. It is exactly the image reported by those who have had near death experiences. At first, a hand rises from a lump of bodies and soon others begin to slowly rise. We see Bridges rising too. Everyone moves very slowly. It feels surreal, like a graveyard with the dead, or their souls, beginning to rise.

We now see Bridges walking toward a bright light at the open end of the fuselage that broke in half when the plane hit the ground. As he moves forward he periodically looks back and smiles, as if saying goodbye to the world, and then walks forward again, as if realizing that he is in passage between this life and an afterlife. It isn't the plane anymore. Look at the picture. There are no seats, no other survivors, no bodies or wreckage; nothing but a clear tunnel with a bright light that pours into the plane. This is the image reported in near death experiences.

Before he is enveloped by the light the film cuts back to Bridges on the dining room floor. He is recovering from choking and regaining consciousness. He is back in this world. He did not die. His spirit or soul was not enveloped by the bright white light at the end of the tunnel. Without saying anything about a belief in an afterlife, or Bridges' religiosity, the movie employs this metaphor of life after death, of something pleasant awaiting Jeff Bridges after his death.

The use of bright light as an image of God is also used earlier in the film when Bridges realizes something is wrong with the airplane: "He can't steer, we're going down." With the steering mechanism out of control, Bridges knows the plane will crash and he will probably die. We see a bright light shining on his face and he says to himself, "This is it, this is the moment of your death." It is as if with the realization of his death he has been led to some contact with the other side (the bright light at the end of the tunnel).

The film then shifts for a moment to the light itself as it reflects off his window pane, and cutting back to his face, he now looks calm, contemplative, and at ease, saying to himself, "I am not afraid, I have no fear." In this cinematic epiphany Bridges has gone from panic and fear of crashing ("He can't steer, we're going down") to a shock-induced realization of his own mortality ("This is it, the moment of your death") to realizing the possibility of something like life after death ("I am not afraid, I have no fear").

God Is Like...

Perhaps one reason today's robust religious imagery, such as the light in *Fearless,* is not more readily recognized is the very literal approach that is often taken to conceiving, visualizing, or in our case screening, God. This may derive from the emphasis placed upon the idea of God as above and beyond the existing world rather than immanent in the people, places, and events of the world. As a result visual representations of God appear not only impossible but often seem sacrilegious, since no particular picture can grasp God's transcendent quality. To such an outlook we would like to counter with a more metaphoric perspective. We begin with a very basic, and we think reasonable, assumption: God, should she or he exist, is, by definition, infinite, hence not representable in three dimensions. Therefore, all God talk, all God images, all God stained glass windows and paintings, and, of course, all God appearances in the movies are—of necessity—nothing but ways of saying God is like this or not like that. Since God is nonrepresentable, all representations are analogies. There simply can be no literal visualization of God. All pictures of God—including God in the movies— have to be works of the human imagination, realized in historically contingent and culturally specific symbols, images, and stories. Following David Tracy's[2] account of how we describe God, we suggest that the analogical religious imagination constructs a mental algorithm when it wants to describe God that goes something to the effect, "God is like…" where the comparison of something in this world is inserted into the equation that has attributes with which we try to describe God. The specific worldly attributes and comparisons are drawn from the culture and historical period of storyteller and moviemaker. From this perspective, no one image of God is inherently more accurate or literal than any other, assuming a well-meaning effort at trying to describe a transcendent God in the colors, shapes, forms, and images of a here-and-now world. A Catholic picture of, or story about, God cannot be better or worse than a Jewish or Protestant story. Aesthetic considerations may make the stained glass windows of a Gothic cathedral beautiful, but not more Godlike or religious than Michelangelo's painted Sistine Chapel ceiling, or Audrey Hepburn in the movie *Always*. In this Steven Spielberg film, Richard Dreyfuss dies when his plane crashes while fighting forest fires. We may not be sure whether he lived or died as he is seen walking in a burned-out forest of smoldering trees. But when he comes upon Audrey Hepburn dressed in white standing on a small patch of beautiful green grass amid the blackened, burned-out forest she is clearly meant to be God or an angel. She informs Dreyfuss about how he is to go back as a spirit and aid the living the way others before had helped him. At first glance one could say: Audrey Hepburn as God? That can't be, makes no sense, and maybe is even sacrilegious. Perhaps. But think again in the analogical mode. Put yourself in the shoes of the filmmakers trying to create a visualization of God. What can they do? What should they show on the screen?

Should God look like Michelangelo's bearded man from his 1511 painting *The Creation of Adam*? Possibly. But remember this is no more accurate a picture than Audrey Hepburn. What to do? Imagine for a moment the moviemakers engage in the "God is like…" analogy exercise and plug in Audrey Hepburn, not because she is literally God, but because in trying to assert the most highly valued human attributes as an analogy for the highest attributes of God, Audrey Hepburn seems a very good comparison. God is like Audrey Hepburn because she is like love, beauty, caring, grace, and tenderness and God is like love, beauty, grace, and caring. Certain images, of course, are so customary that they are taken for granted as appropriate pictures of God. While these traditional images persist the religious imagination is continually creating new images, like Audrey Hepburn, or, for that matter, George Burns who played God in *Oh, God!*, or even the bright light at the end of the tunnel in *Fearless*.

The mistake is to take any of these analogies literally. In that case George Burns' portrayal of God as a wisecracking little old man in yachting cap and windbreaker could easily be seen as a kind of sacrilege. Consider, though, another picture of God: the well-known image of another older man, the powerful one in flowing robes and white beard reaching out to touch the hand of man in Michelangelo's *The Creation of Adam*.

Is this any more realistic or religious an image of God than George Burns in yachting cap and windbreaker? Michelangelo's depiction may be aesthetically superior, but it cannot be any more accurate. A small man with a boating cap vs. a more muscular man with white beard. Two images. Two human efforts at describing the indescribable.

Now let's apply the "God is like…" equation to the Michelangelo and George Burns images. What is being said when God is like Michelangelo's muscular man with white beard? Obviously someone who is strong and powerful, both acceptable descriptions of God. Now let us insert George Burns into the equation. What does this describe? If God is like George Burns he is someone who is loveable, tender, good, approachable, and cares about the world. Now, is there anything sacrilegious about that? No, of course not. Then why is the George Burns God possibly sacrilegious? The only way would be to take George Burns literally as God and not as an analogy for the kindness, love, concern, compassion, and a hundred other wonderful adjectives everyone would agree describe the idea of God.

Both of these images, then, are simply human ways of grasping at some of the attributes of God, and both are produced by different societies in different historical times and at different levels of technological development. Change the historical period and one could ask: would Michelangelo make movies if he were alive today and would George Lucas or Steven Spielberg paint if they lived in sixteenth-century Italy? Maybe; who knows? The important point is that one form of religious imagination should not be privileged over any another. That God is powerful and strong and friendly and approachable are both legitimate descriptions. The human imagination is constantly searching for comparisons with things it knows about to press into metaphoric service in the act of God describing.

Describing God through analogy does not begin with movie images. It starts in the beginning. For example, in the stories of Genesis Jacob wrestles with God—and we mean wrestles as in grabbing legs and arms and tussling with God.

> And Yaakov was left alone. Now a man wrestled with him until the coming up of dawn. When he saw that he could not prevail against him, he touched the socket of his thigh; the socket of Yaakov's thigh had been dislocated as he wrestled with him. Then he said let me go, for dawn has come up!
>
> But he said: I will not let you go unless you bless me. He said to him: What is your name? And he said: Yaakov.
>
> Then he said: Not as Yaakov/Heel-Sneak shall your name be henceforth uttered but rather as Yisrael/God-Fighter for you have fought with God and men and have prevailed.[3]

Now, do we interpret this picturing, or screening, of God in a literal sense? Do we say, that's silly, no one can wrestle with God; Genesis isn't a branch of the World Wrestling Federation. No, we see this as an analogy, and correctly look for the deeper meanings contained in this story of a man wrestling with God. This same outlook also needs to be applied to all stories and images of God, no matter whether a little old man (*Oh, God!*), a beautiful woman (*Always, All That Jazz*) or something as abstract as a puff of white cloud in a blue sky (*Truly, Madly, Deeply*).

Picturing, or in the movies, screening God, is not new. Rembrandt painted Jacob's story as a man wrestling with another man who is wearing bird wings to signify the divine. So does an early thirteenth-century English painting which also has a halo around the head of the man with whom Jacob is wrestling.

Now consider another image, or in the case of movies, a screening, of Jacob wrestling God taken from the movie *Jacob's Ladder* starring Tim Robbins. Here the picture does not involve men or women with bird wings. Here God is depicted as a chiropractor named Louis played by Danny Aiello. When he gives Jacob Singer (Robbins) a chiropractic adjustment he appears to be very much wrestling with Jacob.

In this movie there are other hints that Danny Aiello is playing God or an angel of God. Some are quite explicit: "You know you look like an angel Louis....you're a savior" says Jacob, to which Louis replies, "I know." Later he rescues Jacob from a hellish-looking hospital and takes him back for another chiropractic adjustment (more wrestling with God?). Here with a light hanging from the ceiling that forms a halo over Louis' head, Jacob says, "I was in Hell, Louis....I don't want to die" and Aiello replies, "I'll see what I can do about it." Later their discussion turns to death and how it is to be approached. Louis says, "The only thing that burns in hell is the part of you that won't let go of your life, your memories, your attachments....If you're frightened of dying and you're holding on, the devil will be tearing at you. But if you've made your peace then the devils are really angels freeing you." This is very much a conversation between Jacob and his God about how to approach death.

While God in the form of a chiropractor may be new, wearing a halo isn't, as seen in the thirteenth-century English painting of God and Jacob wrestling.

In the same Genesis story Jacob also dreams of a ladder connecting heaven and earth with God's messengers going up and down.

> Yaakov went out from Be'er-Sheva and went toward Harran, and encoun-
> tered a certain place. He had to spend the night there, for the sun had come
> in. Now he took one of the stones of the place and set it at his head and lay
> down in that place. And he dreamt. Here, a ladder was set up on the earth,
> its top reaching the heavens, and here: messengers of God were going up
> and down on it.[4]

This story of Jacob's ladder has also been visually represented in multiple ways. In the Gutenberg Bible (1450-1550) and in a seventeenth-century English raised silk embroidery God's messengers are represented as men and women with bird's wings on their backs.

In the movie the ladder is a staircase in Jacob Singer's home and God's messenger is now represented as Jacob Singer's deceased son. At the end of the movie, Jacob Singer seems finally at peace about his coming death and goes home to sit in his living room and let go of memories and attachments to family Louis had recommended. Rising from the living room couch, and disbelieving somewhat, he sees his deceased young son sitting on the first step of the staircase. Jacob slowly walks toward him, and his son says, "It's OK....come on, let's go up." Jacob peacefully agrees, and his son takes his hand and they slowly ascend the staircase, which like the fuselage in *Fearless,* is bathed in light at the other end. When they reach the top they disappear into the engulfing white light. It is as if Jacob Singer has died and gone to heaven. The film then cuts to Vietnam where doctors, having failed to save Jacob's life, pronounce him dead. Has he died and ascended to an afterlife, as in going up the stairs? Or, has he just died, with no afterlife? The interpretation is left open.

Again like *Fearless* or *Always* this movie is not religious in any formal sense nor do its characters seem to have any particular religious persuasion. Yet in all these movies the religious imagination is not only alive and well, but has created a sumptuous feast of visual imagery of God, heaven, and angels.

It would appear, then, that as many the religious imaginations, as many the images of God. God has been a muscular man with a flowing white beard and a little man with a golf cap. God has been someone Jacob wrestles with and someone Jerry Landers (John Denver in *Oh, God!*) talks to in a supermarket. God has also been a beautiful woman and an incandescent white light. Some of these images may be more aesthetically pleasing, but more religious, beloved, and generative of devotion, probably not. Such images and stories, then, help emancipate the religious imagination. George Burns and Audrey Hepburn as God are sacrilege only if they are taken literally and not seen as human ways of speaking of God's love, approachability, kindness, and concern. These images of God are no more sacrilegious than the story of a man who wrestles with God or pictures with men and women having bird's wings as God's angels. People simply make their images; they do their best at representing what they think God is about. In our time it is not necessarily paintings, Sistine Chapels, stained glass cathedral windows, but celluloid images on silver screens and it may not be men and women with bird's wings but beautiful women and loving, caring older men. There is an old saying about honoring your own incarnation, and there is an analog here. We need to honor our own religious imagination. It is there, on the screen, right in front of us, being expressed every weekend. Not in every movie, not all the time, and not always as the central subject, but there to be seen and appreciated.

A.J.B.

Notes

1. Gore Vidal, *Screening History*, Cambridge: Harvard University Press, 1992, P.2, 5.
2. For discussion of imagining God in more transcendent vs. more immanent ways see David Tracy, *The Analogical Imagination*. New York, Crossroad, 1982.
3. Quoted from *The Five Books of Moses Schocken Bible* in Bill Moyers, *Genesis*, New York: Doubleday, P. 277-278.
4. Quoted from *The Five Books of Moses Schocken Bible* in Bill Moyers, *Genesis*, Doubleday, 1996, p. 226.

3

Always a Lover: Audrey Hepburn
as Lady Wisdom

"If God were really like Audrey Hepburn, I'd have no trouble believing in God."
—an undergraduate

The hotshot pilot kisses his girlfriend goodbye, yells that he loves her, slips into the cockpit of his Martin B-26 (Marauder), slides the transparent hatch over his head, taxis down the runway and takes off. His buddy Al, flying a PBY amphibious flying boat (Catalina), is a few minutes ahead of him on the bombing run. The infantry on the ground give Al directions on the target; he zooms close to the ground, releases his ordinance, begins to pull up, and hits a tree. One of his engines catches fire. He yanks the release on the fire extinguishing liquid. The flame dies momentarily (as it always does in films like this) and then explodes again. By his own admission, he is "screwed."

Then Pete, the hotshot pilot, puts his Marauder into a steep dive, roars over the "Cat" and releases his fire retardant (the enemy in this film are forest fires, not German or Japanese pilots). The fire in the Cat's engine goes out, its feathered prop spins idly. Al thanks Pete and shouts at him to pull out. On the ground the head of the infantry (firefighters) shouts the same thing. The Marauder pulls out of the dive. Al and Pete shout joyfully. Then the wing tank on the Marauder explodes, the plane tumbles towards earth. Pete looks out the cockpit window at his coming death.

The scene cuts to the control tower where Dorinda, the pilot's girlfriend, stares glumly out of the window. Pete had promised to retire.

27

This was his last flight before he chose some other and safer form of aviation. Now it was his last flight ever.

Yet the next scene shows Pete, in his flight jacket, cockily swaggering through the burnt-out forest, whistling a confident tune. The sky turns blue, a deer leaps by him, he is impressed by the rapid change. No more smoke, no more fire. Then he emerges into a clearing. In the center of it is a patch of green, a chair, and a woman in white leaning against a tree.

"Hi, Pete," she says, "That was some show."

Her name, she tells him, is Hap. (Happiness? The source of all happiness? What else?)

Pete swaggers into the clearing and admits that it was indeed some show. She beckons him to a barber's chair, tucks him into the required white sheet, and begins to cut his hair—his girlfriend had insisted the day before that he needed a haircut. We get a closer look at her. She's wearing a white ribbed sweater and white slacks. Her hair is tied up in a knot. She's very attractive, neither young nor old, fragile with a lovely neck, charming with a radiant smile, tender and gentle with an appealingly quirky voice. She is also very much in charge—a mother, a nurse, a wife.

Pete observes proudly that it was some explosion that brought his plane down. She agrees that it was a real fireball. He reflects on the explosion and comments that either he's crazy or he's dead.

"You're not crazy, Pete," Hap says solemnly as she continues with the haircut.

Then she explains that Pete is now spirit, wind, and that just as he was taught how to respond instinctively to the crises of flying by the inspiration of someone else, now it is his job to do the same thing for someone else.

Suddenly they are not in the forest but in a field of grain and a plane is flying over them. The pilot is the one he must inspire. Then they are on the tarmac of a runway, a plane is landing, Pete must begin his new —and temporary—life as "spirit." He will shortly discover that the new pilot is also courting his girlfriend.

The doctrine taught by Hap is a variation on two Catholic doctrines —the Communion of Saints and Purgatory. The former teaches that the boundaries between the living and the dead are thin and that they can influence one another. The latter teaches that there is a time after our lives on this earth are over when we can still do things for people on earth as we straighten out our destiny. Whether the writers and the director of the film knew these doctrines explicitly does not matter (I doubt that they did). For both doctrines are based on human instincts which are older than Christianity and which seem to permeate the human condition.

The film is *Always*. Pete is played by Richard Dreyfuss, Dorinda by Holly Hunter, Al by John Goodman, and Hap, the woman in white, is Audrey Hepburn in her final movie role. As Richard Graves said in the Arts and Entertainment *Biography* of Ms. Hepburn it was her biggest role because she played God.

I had no intention of watching the film. I have always been able to contain my enthusiasm for both Mr. Dreyfuss and Ms. Hunter. The reviewers didn't like it, Roger Ebert arguing that it was one of Steven Spielberg's few failures.

But then someone called me (presumably my nephew Sean who monitors films for me) and told me that I had to see it because Audrey Hepburn played God. None of the critics seemed to have noticed this; even Roger Ebert said that she was an angel. However, no matter how bad the film was, I knew I had to see it. Immediately.

It was my annual term at the University of Arizona. Even though there was snow at the 3,000-foot level (and I lived at the 2,500-foot level), I promptly abandoned my computer and drove to the nearest theater where *Always* was playing. If Spielberg was using the metaphor of Audrey Hepburn as God, this I had to see.

There is a bit of autobiography involved in this compulsion, a compulsion, which dated to the winter of 1953. I attended one of the better seminaries founded in the early nineteenth century. Our rector was a man twenty-five years ahead of his time: he was solving the problems of 1825 with the answers of 1850. We were incarcerated in the seminary from September to June with no time off for good behavior. We were not permitted to go home for Christmas. We did, however, enjoy two weeks off at the end of January and the beginning of February, a time when lay people our age (and whom we were supposed to serve as priests in a couple of years) might be around to trouble our vocations —lay women especially.

There were no newspapers, radio, or television. We could read three magazines, the Jesuit journal *America*, the Benedictine publication *Orate Fratres* (which later became *Worship*), and *Liturgical Arts*. One could be expelled if one was caught with a copy of *Time*.

We were permitted three visiting Sundays each semester – two hours on a Sunday afternoon in classrooms. Heaven help us if we said a word to our families after the two hours were up. Just to keep us honest (no more than three guests) a priest would patrol the classrooms during our brief interlude.

Seminarian's sisters, someone said, were the most beautiful women in the world. Someone else remarked that you often imagined hearing the click of heels on the sidewalk. Is it any wonder that the Church's practice of clerical celibacy is in disarray after such infantile attempts to prepare us for it?

The monotony of the long, cold winter in rural northern Illinois was broken by an occasional movie, also three a semester, though at irregular intervals. The rector loved to keep us guessing with a cat and mouse game he played over whether and when there would be a film and what it would be.

He always searched for films in which there were no women. Sometimes he was less than successful. After *The Red Danube* in which Janet Leigh played a ballerina whom the Communists were trying to kidnap from Vienna, the ancient Jesuit spiritual director harangued us to stay away from the "ballot" when we were home on vacation. It took awhile for me to realize that he meant "ballet" and he was warning us against the temptation to ogle ballerinas as attractive as Ms. Leigh in skimpy costumes. It must be noted that the chances of Catholic seminarians in that era going to a ballet were about as great as their seeking out a kabuki theater.

Anyway, in the winter of 1953, he tempted us with various films whose titles suggested a better cure for insomnia than sheep. Then, without warning, he announced that the film would be *Roman Holiday*. There would be, he observed, lots of scenery of Roman churches, maybe even a shot of the Holy Father.

It must have been after a vacation because I remembered an article I had read about Audrey Hepburn. I warned my classmates that the rector had made an awful mistake, but didn't tell them why because I knew they wouldn't believe me.

There was indeed a lot of Roman scenery in the film, but I don't think any of us noticed it.

So Ms. Hepburn, who was just our age, imprinted herself on the memories of a whole generation of Chicago seminarians. We all fell in love with her, an ethereal young woman with a wonderful smile, an aristocratic imp with a beautiful voice, and light-touch sex appeal far more devastating than Janet Leigh in a ballerina costume. In a minor way she was for us like the "sea-bird" woman in Joyce's *Portrait of the Artist*. She was an image of woman that the Jesuit spiritual director could not possibly attack (and he did not), a woman who was a challenge indeed, but not a threat.

We were not the only ones who fell in love with her. A whole generation of moviegoers of both sexes did the same. She represented light and brightness and laughter and love. I saw all her films after *Roman Holiday* (which won the Academy Award)—*Funny Face, Breakfast at Tiffany's, War and Peace, Charade, Sabrina, My Fair Lady, Wait Until Dark, Robin and Marian*. Somehow she was always airy grace and light-hearted gaiety. She grew old as we did, but somehow was forever young.

Audrey Hepburn as a metaphor for God! How delicious!

I would never have imagined such an image in 1953, though perhaps I would have reacted favorably to it even then because I understood that all human beauty and human grace disclosed God's beauty. But by 1989 I realized that all God-talk is metaphorical and that God's loveliness can be reflected just as well by a special young woman as by an old man with white hair and a beard—indeed more effectively reflected.

So off I went to the Century Park theater on a dark winter afternoon to learn whether Spielberg had the ingenuity and the good taste to cast her as God. When I came out of the theater I discovered three inches of snow on my car. I didn't mind. At sixty Audrey Hepburn was as attractive (if in a different way) as she had been at twenty-four and a brilliant metaphor for an always attractive God.

Indeed, even in pictures in the *Biography* taken when she was dying, the beauty of *Roman Holiday* is still there, devastated but still luminous, as were her words of consolation to her family which might have well come from Hap in *Always*. She had come on a long and tragic journey from the teenager in occupied Holland where she carried messages for the underground and almost starved because of Nazi cruelty[1] to a good-will ambassador who worked for starving children all over the world. Each of us must walk our own tragic path. Ms. Hepburn showed in both films and real life how to walk that path with dignity, elegance, and luminosity.

Always was a remake of a 1944 film *A Guy Named Joe* which both Spielberg and Dreyfuss adored—the latter had watched it thirty-five times. Spencer Tracy had played Pete, Ward Bond was Al, Van Johnson was Ted (the new pilot), Irene Dunne was Dorinda, and Lionel Barrymore was the "General," the heavenly figure who explained to Pete what death meant. The men were combat aviators. Pete sacrificed his life to save his friend Al and then had to help Ted to become a skilled combat pilot and tolerate his romance with Dorinda. In *A Guy Named Joe* the deity (Barrymore) is in military uniform and is called "The General." In Spielberg's remake there is not only a gender change, but a change of the whole atmosphere of contact with the Ultimate. No one, however, ever suggested that Barrymore was not God. Doubt about Ms. Hepburn as the God character misses the subtle theological insight that Spielberg adds to *A Guy Named Joe*. Granted that the shift might be motivated by Spielberg's notorious propensity to be politically correct, it also reflects the valid feminist insight that God is, as Cardinal Nicholas of Cusa remarked, a combination of opposites, neither male nor female and both male and female.

The original screenplay was written by Dalton Trumbo, one of the film writers who was blacklisted during the McCarthy era (Joseph, not Eugene) for suspected Communist leanings. Spielberg acknowledges Trumbo's original script in the credits, perhaps another example of his obsession with political preaching.

The critics of that era ridiculed it—"an icky romantic comedy-drama with strong propaganda intent," "melodrama, farce, fake philosophy." James Agee was particularly devastating, "It neatly obtunds death's sting as ordinary people experience it by not only assuming but photographing a good, busy, hearty, hereafter." He added, "Joe's affability in the afterlife is enough to discredit the very idea that death in combat amounts to anything more than getting a freshly pressed uniform."

Perhaps. But since neither Agee nor anyone else has been there, who is to say what the afterlife might be like. Those who may have been on its fringes in near death experiences have a different view.

In any event, unlike the critics, Spielberg and Dreyfuss thought it was worth making again. Unfortunately, their attempt to create the atmosphere and tone of a 1940s film in a 1980s setting didn't quite work, perhaps because of too slavish an imitation of Trumbo's script. The film was not very good. But the implicit theology of Audrey Hepburn as God made it worth seeing. Dreyfuss in the Audrey Hepburn *Biography* describes those who were involved in planning the film sitting around and discussing who should play the God role. Finally, Spielberg exclaimed, "Audrey Hepburn!" Everyone, according to Dreyfuss, thought it was a perfect choice. One would dearly like to know what went on in Spielberg's imagination at the time he chose Hepburn for the role.

Could God really be like her?

Or could God possibly be any different?

My students, always uneasy with metaphors for God, are especially disconcerted when I suggest that she really is God, which is to say the metaphor that the filmmakers choose for God. (In these essays my students act as surrogates for those readers who might well have the same objections.) Like Roger Ebert, they want to think of her as an angel. One could argue that in the Hebrew scriptures the *Malek Yahweh* is nothing more than Yahweh revealing Himself to humans. So whether Ms. Hepburn is an angel or not is immaterial. Even if she is an angel, she is still an appropriate metaphor for God and the issue becomes what aspect of her is particularly powerful.

Students tend to resist the notion that any human can represent God. I ask those who are Christian about Jesus. Jesus, they reply promptly (and heretically) was not human, He was God. All right, I say to them, if you don't like the word "metaphor," what about the word "sacrament?" They back off on that. It sounds like it might be all right (particularly to Catholic students), but they're not sure I'm not playing a word game with them.

Whatever their religious background, the students are fundamentalists (with a small "f" please note) who want to divorce God utterly from creation. They cannot accept the startling notion that the only way we know God is through God's creatures. Admittedly such knowledge is speculative and analogical (or metaphorical), but it is all we have. Either we do not talk about God at all or we engage in comparisons with God's creatures, knowing that the comparisons are inadequate but that they give us hints.

If we are to compare God to creatures then why not to the highest of his creatures (about whom we know anything) humans? Are such comparisons to be limited only to men and old men at that?

(In fact, God is eternal and therefore always young).

Students still don't like the argument. There's always a couple of young people (women usually) who insist that they have twelve years of Catholic school and know that God is not a woman. Bad reflection on Catholic education I tell them. Can God be compared to a woman, I ask, especially since the verb "is" means "is like?"

They still don't want to give up the image of the old man with a beard.

They are particularly disturbed when God is compared to a sexually attractive woman. (Even students are willing to admit that Audrey Hepburn in *Always* is sexually attractive, a major concession from young people. I do not however tell them that she was sixty when the film was made. That would be too much.) Sexual attraction, they contend, is lust and it's wrong to think of God in terms of lust.

That's heresy too, Puritanism if you are Protestant, Jansenism if you are Catholic. God makes it clear in the Jewish Scriptures that He yearns passionately for his people. St. Paul compares the desire between man and woman to the desire between Jesus and His church. Jansenist (or Puritan) fundamentalists still don't like it. Then someone sticks up a hand and announces that if God really is like Audrey Hepburn, then God is certainly worth believing in. This insight generally carries the day. Hap's tenderness with Pete is irresistible. If God is really like that, then it's very good news indeed.

But, isn't she really too easy, too "soft," too kind? some intransigent fundamentalist asks?

What sort of God, is it then, for which Audrey Hepurn is a metaphor, a sacrament, a revelation? What kind of God broke through into Steven Spielberg's imagination when he decided to cast her in the role?

Pete discovers that Ted is in love with Dorinda. He intervenes to stop the romance. He reminds her—though she can't see him and is unaware of his presence—that she is his girl. Though she is in love with Ted, she cannot let go of her memory of Pete. The budding love is arrested and Pete is bounced back to the little meadow in the burned-out forest. Hap is sitting on the ground, leaning against a tree, one arm across her knee, her head propped in her other hand. She is, one senses, not altogether happy with Pete.

I told you, she says mildly, that your life is over and that any attempt to bring it back is a waste of spirit. Pete does not accept the rebuke. Hap, he says, you didn't tell me the whole story. You didn't tell me that this guy was going to fall in love with Dorinda. Hap doesn't back down. You're a good man, she insists, that's why we sent you back. We don't do that with the others. You never told her you loved her. You have to free her before you're free yourself.

Note that three new dimensions are added to the picture of Hap (Happiness?). First she uses the "we" of majesty like popes, and emperors, and God in the Genesis story. Second, she says that there are others who don't get the chance to undo their mistakes. Third, she implies that once Dorinda is free, so too will Pete be free.

For what?

She doesn't say. For whatever comes next for him. Pete smiles. Now he understands. The issue is to free Dorinda because he loves her and then to go on while she goes on. That seems to be enough.

The rest of the film is unbearably hokey. Dorinda steals Ted's plane (now an A-20 Invader, if anyone cares) and, in a night flight with Pete whispering in her ear, creates a path through the fire for trapped fire fighters. Then he tells her that he loves her and she seems to understand. The hydraulics fail and she crash-lands in a lake. She is ready to die, even eager to die. Pete pulls her out of the plane (which in the theory of the film, he ought not to be able to do) and urges her to go on with her life. She wades ashore and strides down the runway (which is conveniently right next to the lake). Pete watches admiringly from the edge of the runway and the film fades out.

As saccharine as the ending is, the lesson Hap was trying to teach is driven home: one must not cling to life. One must free others so that their lives go on. Only by letting go will we find freedom for ourselves. He who seeks his life will lose it, he who loses his life will find it.

Pete has experienced Purgatory, though neither he nor Hap uses the name. Now he goes on happily to whatever comes next.

In her second scene Hap refutes the charge that she is "soft." She is displeased with Pete and tells him so. He tries to argue back and she vigorously refutes him. She continues to be affectionate and tender, but also firm and even tough. It is no easy task for a lover to be both tender and tough, to deliver a reprimand and still be affectionate. Yet it is in the nature of love that we try for such combinations and that we expect those who love us to do the same. Nevertheless, we have no such expectations of God. We figure that if God is displeased with us, He must speak with thunder and lightning, storms and waves, and heaven-rending pyrotechnics. Once more, we engage in the patent heresy of denying to God appealing characteristics we find in humans.

The question is not whether God's displeasure with us is like Hap's in *Always* but whether any other kind of allegedly divine anger comes from God at all. Is God like Hap? How can God not be like Hap?

Are we more likely or less to fall in love with a human who can combine tenderness and toughness in exactly the right proportions and

become even more appealing in the process? If we attribute such se-
ductiveness to human lovers, why do we deny it to a possible divine
lover?

Perhaps because we are iconoclasts and want no images of God in
our religion. Iconoclasm was a heresy, but that does not make it un-
popular. Alas, for the iconoclastic temptation, humans are bodily spirits and we cannot help imagining God. If there is a choice between
imagining an almost irrationally furious God and a God who combines
the tenderness and the toughness, the firmness and the appeal of Hap,
how can anyone imagine that the former is the better metaphor?

In the Hebrew scriptures there is a figure called "Wisdom." The word
means many things, especially in the various books of Wisdom, but it is
often a personification of characteristics of God. It is a feminine noun
and the personified Wisdom is often a feminine person. Scripture scholars reflect these aspects of Wisdom today when they refer to her as
Lady Wisdom. In so doing they do not read feminism into the text of
the bible where it is not there, but rather, with the illumination of the
insights of feminism, recognize in the text meanings which they had
not hitherto perceived. (The French philosopher Paul Ricoeur calls this
the "meaning in front of the text.") Such meanings, perhaps intended
only unconsciously by the author of the text, are uncovered by prayer-
ful reading of the text from the perspective of our accumulated insights
into the nature of the human condition.

Father Roland Murphy of the Carmelite order in an important presi-
dential address to the Society for Biblical Literature, argues persua-
sively that Lady Wisdom represents God as God invites us through the
beauty of creation. God is not only the One who creates everything, but
also the one who appeals to our hungers with the beauty that has been
created. Indeed the God who invites, who seduces us with beauty, may
be the most appropriate image of God and the most powerful theology
of God may well come from reflection on this image.

A poet's reflection on the image that has exploded in her head can
never be as immediate, as powerful, as luminous, as embracing as the
image itself. As much as one would like to hear from Steven Spielberg
what went on in his head when he cast Audrey Hepburn as God, it is
most unlikely that he could explain in such a way that his explanation
would not dim the luminosity of his vision. Better not to ask why.

But he saw the figure of Lady Wisdom even if he had never heard of
the name. He perceived a brilliant contrast between Lionel Barrymore

and Audrey Hepburn, between the God who creates and the God who invites. The change in our consciousness about the role of women in the last half century made it possible to see God as Lady Wisdom more clearly than Dalton Trumbo and his director did. Moreover, Lady Wisdom, a mother, a spouse, a nurse, a sister,[2] a mature lover, is a God image which is more acceptable today than she would have been half a century ago—some net progress in the human condition.

To reduce Lady Wisdom to an angel (as we understand angels, not as Hebrew Scripture understands them) is to diminish and distort Spielberg's poetic vision. If God is Lady Wisdom, if God invites through beauty and charm and tenderness, then Audrey Hepburn as Hap is as good a metaphor as one is likely to find.

But, finally, is God really that way? Only maybe more attractive, more appealing, more charming, more tender?

If someone comes along and claims to be God and isn't that way, pay that person no heed. It's not God.

Lady Wisdom

(Based on Audrey Hepburn as God in the film *Always*)

When you wake up from surgery, a skillful nurse—
Compassionate, sensitive—a distant light,
A promise of peace and reassurance,
A loving mother to tuck you in at night.
No longer is there any need to hide,
All is seen and long ago remitted
A sympathetic judge, a case already tried
And a verdict given—"you're acquitted!"

He's not a great accountant in the sky
Nor an old monsignor with a walking cane
Who waits to chase us quickly off to hell,
But a long-loved spouse who wipes away our pain
And draws us to her breasts that we may cry—
In her embrace things always turn out well.

A.M.G.

Notes

1. And the ineptitude of General Bernard Law Montgomery and the British First Army who failed to take advantage of Operation Market Garden and stole defeat from the jaws of victory.
2. All of which were considered to be appropriate images in the Middle Ages, which were much less uptight about metaphors than we are.

4

Life, Love, and *All That Jazz*:
Jessica Lange and the Passion of God

All That Jazz begins with the first of four stories that create the complex fabric of a brilliant and intricate film. Fosse weaves the four stories in and out with enormous technical skills:

1. The dialogue between Joe Gideon (Roy Scheider before he assumed his submarine command) and Angelique (Jessica Lange);
2. The story of the last days of Joe Gideon's compulsive, reckless, and self-destructive life;
3. The story in a film Gideon is editing called *The Standup* in which Fosse tries to explain Elizabeth Kübler-Ross's paradigm of death and dying;
4. The story of Joe's Gideon's heart surgery.

In the opening scene Joe Gideon is in a darkened office with a radiant woman in bridal garb (including a large hat and veil). They are reviewing his life and the mess he has made of it. The woman in white is tough, she asks pointed questions and makes critical observations. Joe cheerfully admits that he's a jerk, an incorrigible womanizer, an obsessive worker, a man who lives off drugs. Yet the woman remains affectionate, even tender. She is in fact far more sympathetic to Joe Gideon than he is to himself.

The cutting between the various stories goes on at a frantic pace. The first time I saw the film (in the spring of 1979) I was baffled by what was going on. Then, maybe in the second scene with Scheider and Lange, I realized that Joe Gideon was dead and this dialogue was what Catholics called when I was growing up his "particular judgment." We were taught that we were judged both at the end of our lives and at the final,

39

sumptuous Last Judgment. Some of the nuns turned the metaphor into an allegory. God would be the judge, our guardian angel would act for defense, the devil would be the prosecutor, and Mary the Mother of Jesus would appear as a character witness. In some versions of this allegory, the angels and saints would constitute the jury while in others God would be both judge and jury.

As experienced by Bob Fosse, however, he himself was the prosecutor and Angelique was judge, jury, defense attorney, and character witness. She made no excuses for him, but she loved him just the same. He was indeed a jerk, a bum, a wastrel, a cad. Still he was lovable.

So he's dead, I thought, and this is his judgment. Is Fosse suggesting that God might be like Jessical Lange?

I was familiar with Kübler-Ross's work, I had read a manuscript of some of Dr. Raymond Moody's work (which later appeared in his *Life after Life*), I had written three years earlier a book called *The Mary Myth* in which I had argued that the sociological function of devotion to Mary in Catholicism was to be a sacrament of the mother love of God. In that book I had traced the themes of the womanliness of God (who is a combination of opposites, a *composito oppositorum), as minor keys in the Jewish and Christian heritage.*

As Fosse wove his four stories in and out I began to sort out the themes and figure out what he was up to. The most astonishing aspect of the film was that Fosse was suggesting that God (or at least Death and the Judge) might be something like a tender and sexy woman. Jessica Lange might be a metaphor for God.

Of all the metaphors for God to be found in the movies, none is more startling, more original, and more profound than the image of Jessica Lange as God in Bob Fosse's remarkable (Cannes prize-winning) film *All That Jazz*. Writing out of his own experience of near death and with only a minimum of religious vocabulary, Fosse approaches death and God not as a religiously convinced man and certainly not as a propagandist, but as a thoroughly secular human being trying to make sense out of his own tormented life and his own experience of death. The result is a daring metaphor for the possibility that God is not merely love, but passionate love, a metaphor elaborated without the slightest concern for its theological orthodoxy or its basis in scripture and tradition— about all of which matters Fosse could not have cared less.

In fact, in both the Jewish and Christian scriptures, God appears as a passionate lover. Many fundamentalist and evangelical folk find that metaphor difficult to accept. They want the statement "God is Love" interpreted in an equivocal sense. Love has a totally different meaning, they argue, when predicated of God and of humans. Human erotic attraction can therefore tell us nothing about God. However, if divine love is not at all like human love, then why use it as a metaphor? Why would St. Paul call it the "great metaphor?"

So in the Christian tradition (especially the Catholic Christian tradition) the love poetry of the Song of Songs is applied to the relationship between humans and God. However, normally the image is of human passion for God, much more rarely does it imply a reciprocal passion of God for humans. Fosse's innovation is to depict the passionately loving God as a woman.

Images of the motherhood of God are a low-key component of the Christian tradition. Lady Wisdom is a figure in the Jewish scriptures. But a passionately loving woman, a woman who finds humans erotically attractive? Such imagery is generally thought to be too shocking to express.

We so desperately want to deny God passion. Even more desperately do we want to deny God womanly passion. Male attraction for a spouse may be tolerated in descriptions of God. In Exodus 21 God is depicted as saying that he is a "passionate" God, with the word usually translated as "jealous" though in the only other place the word is used in the Hebrew Scriptures it describes the emotions of a newly married groom for his bride. However, the passion a bride may experience for her groom, is somehow deemed unworthy, perhaps even unspeakable, as a metaphor for God. One can only conclude that, while manly passion is tolerable, womanly passion is by its very nature evil.

Even the Catholic tradition which believes that everything is grace, that all created realities are sacramental, that is to say, revelatory, becomes skittish at the suggestion that womanly passion may be revelatory. One can think of two possible reasons for this skittishness—passion is evil in itself or women are evil in themselves. Or, arguably, both are true.

If my students are any reflection of attitudes which are more widely accepted, women are even less likely to believe that the attraction Angelique (Jessica Lange) feels for God is a valid metaphor for God. A sexually attractive and sexually attracted woman cannot be sacramental, cannot be a metaphor for God.

Precisely because he was utterly unreligious and utterly unfamiliar with the hang-ups of the religious heritages, Bob Fosse had no problem casting Jessica Lange (his one-time mistress) in the role of a God possibility. In his brush with death he had encountered an utterly enthralling lover who reminded him of the passionately tender women in his life. Who but Ms. Lange to play the role?

God, the Catholic renaissance theologian Cardinal Nicholas of Cusa (also called on occasion Cusana) wrote is a combination of opposites, a *conincidentia oppositorum*. In God all contrary characteristics are combined, light and darkness, mercy and justice, male and female. It would follow from this insight of Cusana that it is legitimate to picture God as either male or female depending on our devotional needs. About a third of Americans imagine God as either mother or equally mother and father. Morever, this image did not in our early research correlate with either gender or age (more recently it is stronger among men and women under thirty). Apparently the metaphor of God as woman has been lurking in the population for a long time and religious leadership has not noticed it. As a woman of my generation remarked to me, "anyone who has held her new-born child and been filled with love for that little creature to whom she has given life knows that God feels that way about us."

Catholicism has finessed the issue with its devotion to Mary, the Mother of Jesus who reflects the womanly dimensions of God to the Catholic faithful and hence is enormously popular with them. St. Bernard of Clairvaux summarized this popularity when he wrote, "If you fear the father, go to the son; if you fear the son, go to the mother." Moreover the medieval love poetry written to the mother of Jesus contains barely disguised erotic overtones.

The point here is not that one must imagine God as a woman and indeed as a passionately loving woman, but that one may; religious metaphors are opportunities, not obligations. Religious conservatives shout in horror that the image of God as woman will "confuse the ordinary" people. We know from the data that it will not confuse at least a third of them. My own experience is that once one explains Cusana to them, most laity people are delighted rather than confused. Indeed, the fear of "confusion" is usually nothing more than a projection of the conservatives own rigidity.

Nonetheless Fosse's imagery seems as shocking to many today as it was when the film first appeared twenty years ago. God is not "physical" my students tell me. God's love is pure, not "lustful." There's not much one can say in debate against such Puritanism or Jansenism. Its most basic assumptions rule out the possibility that human love can tell us anything about God's love. The physical is in itself evil. Human desire is inherently lustful. What a terrible mistake God made in creating sexual differentiation!

People are free to choose the metaphors they like. If Jessica Lange is a shocking metaphor to some folks then they are utterly within their rights when they reject the metaphor. But they have no right to deny the metaphor to others. In our research on Catholic young people some time ago, we found that the womanly metaphor for God had no religious or human payoff for young women, but substantial payoff for young men. The latter were more likely to pray, to be socially active, to be concerned about the environment, to attend Mass, and to report sexually fulfilling marriages (if they were married). There was also in this data set a strong correlation between positive images of Mary, the Mother of Jesus, and images of the womanly aspect of God.

So, it might be argued, a third of Americans think of God as either mother or equally mother and father, so what? Why offend or confuse the other two-thirds by suggesting this metaphor to the general public? But only a third of Americans think of God as lover or at least equally lover and judge, although the scriptures leave no doubt that God describes himself as a lover. Should we nonetheless refuse to address the metaphor of God as lover because it will offend or confuse the general public?

If one combines three images of God—lover, spouse (as opposed to Master), and mother, 15 percent of Americans (men two percentage points more than women) describe God as a combination of the three. If one combines lover and spouse, then almost a quarter of Americans (men, again, more than women) think of God as both lover and spouse. Thus the image of God as a romantic lover exists in a certain proportion of Americans, with only slight correlations with sex and age.

In another survey, a quarter of Americans (again, men more than women) said that at least sometimes their spouse was like a god to them. If one then asks what set of characteristics distinguishes those with this image from others, the strongest predictor is a factor that emphasizes romance. The next most powerful predictor is one that emphasizes ease at, and delight in, nakedness with spouse.

One can't make the case that images of God as a romantic and passionate lover permeate American society. Quite the contrary, most

Americans would rather imagine God as a master and a judge and a father, understandably, perhaps, given the Calvinist and Puritan attitudes which still permeate American culture. Catholics, whose heritage should make them more tolerant of a wide variety of metaphors for God, are only somewhat more likely to have romantic images of God. However, this imagery correlates more strongly with social, political, and artistic values for Catholics than it does for Protestants.

All one can conclude from the empirical data, however, is that the imagery in *All That Jazz* is not totally foreign to the American population. Indeed for some people it is present and powerful. Perhaps the sharp differences in reactions to the film are based, in part, on the sharp differences in religious imagery which exist among Americans.

So unthinkable is the image of God as a sexually appealing woman and a woman sexually appealed to that most film critics missed it completely (Roger Ebert being a happy exception). In interviews neither Bob Fosse nor Jessica Lange ever referred to the precise nature of "Angelique." Perhaps those who made the film were not sure, not even Fosse himself. I suspect that he did not know whether the reality he experienced in his brush with death was God. He knew that the reality was attractive and loving, very much unlike the skeleton with sickle and much like the women who loved him, especially his wife, his mistress, and his daughter. The woman in white in the film has no name. In the credits she is called "Angelique," doubtless because she is the angel of death. Fosse probably did not know that in the Jewish Scriptures the Angel of the Lord is merely the Lord manifesting Himself in human form. He was utterly innocent of theological, not to say religious sophistication.

Fosse suspected that she might be God and raises the question in the film whether those who view it might have the same suspicions: could God be a passionate lover, a lover who is both passionate in desire for us and arouses passionate desire in us?

For those familiar with the Jewish and Christian scriptures, the answer has to be "yes" to both those questions. However, to Fosse's second questions, can that passionate lover be something like a woman, the answer will seem to many to be less obvious.

One concludes, therefore, that to such folks man can be a useful metaphor for God, but woman cannot.

Fosse does not preach, he does not teach, he does not indoctrinate. He tells a story that ends with a question. He reports an experience with death which astonishes him and which might illumine those with whom he shares his story. The story seems utterly pagan, so pagan, in fact, in some of his dance routines, especially one he calls "Airotica" that it would seem to preclude the possibility of calling the film religious (though at the end of this number, Joe Gideon, his alter ego, attacks meaningless sex in an aside that one has to listen closely to catch). If one defines religion as piety, devotion, doctrinal orthodoxy, then *All That Jazz* is definitely not religious. But if one defines religion as the quest to understand the meaning of life, the nature of death, and identity of God, then *All That Jazz* is profoundly religious—perhaps the most religious film ever made. It is all the more religious precisely because the filmmaker was anything but a religious man before he encountered the Angel of Death.

Since Fosse is dealing with the ultimate human issue—death—in such complex narrative interweaving, the film must be viewed several times if one wishes to tease out the intricate story being told and the nuances of Fosse's tentative answer to the question of who and what is death—and maybe who and what is God. I have watched the film at least a dozen times and find something new in it every time.

The film is autobiographical, a clear-eyed and critical self-examination by the director of his own life. Like all stories which are based on such self-examination, the details are often fictional, but the basic experience is not. Probably someone who reveals himself in a story tells a good deal more (perhaps more than he would want) than he would in a standard nonfiction memoir. You can't hide yourself in a story. Fosse does not hesitate to project himself as a jerk who has wasted his life and his talents and does not deserve to be loved by anyone. All the more surprising to him and to us, therefore, is the fact that "Angelique" loves him—and wants him.

It is not clear that Fosse was familiar with the near death experience (NDE) literature which was only beginning to appear in the late 1970s and which might have been more useful for his purposes than the work of Kübler-Ross. Yet the review of life, the long tunnel, and the figure in light at the end of the tunnel are classic aspects of the NDE. Fosse surely did have a near death experience and wants to tell us about it. Critics like Leonard Maltin who miss that, have missed everything about the film.

As I sat mesmerized by the film on that Sunday afternoon twenty years ago, I wondered whether Fosse was really suggesting that Jessica Lange might be a metaphor for God. There were all kinds of hints.

She knew too much about Joe Gideon to be a mere human. She was too indulgent to be an angel (as indulgent as the Father of the Prodigal Sons [plural deliberate] in the Gospel). She was bathed in radiant light and loved this bum. Who else but God might love such a jerk?

The tip-off came in a cutting sequence between Angelique (whose name I would learn only when the credits came up at the end of the film) and the Standup who is working his way through the Kübler-Ross paradigm. Gideon, now thoroughly fed up with himself, mutters to Angelique that he has never done anything worthwhile.

Angelique is not convinced that he is serious. She banters with him that all the reviews of his work that are piled up on his desk suggest that he has done excellent work. But I've never done anything perfect, he replies. Like making a rose.

Oh, Joe, she says with a chuckle, only God can make a rose!

The film cuts back to Joe Gideon working on cutting the film. The stand-up comedian is working through the Kübler-Ross phases. O God, he shouts, I'm going to die. Immediately after the cry for God we cut back to Angelique who has a rose now wound around her white glove. In that moment, I believe, Bob Fosse tells us his hunch—Angelique might very well be God.

In another scene Joe Gideon has his first heart attack at a rehearsal. We cut back to Angelique and Joe. She has begun to disrobe, to put aside her veil and her dress. Her shoulders are bare. She is wearing some sort of minimal undergarment. She kisses Joe. He backs off. She lets him go. She will only take him as her lover when he is ready to go. Is death the consummation of a love affair? Fosse suggests it might be. A love affair with God?

Maybe.

How much of this symbolism was clear to Fosse when he was making the film? The question cannot be answered and is irrelevant. We cannot require a storyteller in the flush of creativity to understand everything that he is doing. The creative dimension of the personality takes over and rushes madly ahead of the reflecting self. Yet, as Paul Ricoeur has said, there is a meaning in front of a text, a meaning which might not have occurred explicitly to the author but which nonetheless is a legitimate interpretation of the images he offers us.

It is necessary to interpret stories and images, especially if we are critics, professors, students. Yet reflective interpretation always runs the risk of weakening the power and illumination of the image.

Finally, it comes time for Joe Gideon to die definitively during his third surgery. After the first one he continues his reckless behavior, defying death as he has all his life. He experiences a second heart attack and they operate on him again. Finally he has yet another attack, this time without his active defiance of death. The film turns to a fantasy sequence in which Gideon imagines a series of dance numbers for a play about a dying man in surgery, a play in which he will be both the actor and the director.

The first several times around I found these series of dances, like all the others in the film, to be a meaningless distraction. I don't particularly like Broadway dances (I walked out on Fosse's play *Chicago* which I found vulgar, smutty and an insult to my beloved hometown—I also think Sinatra singing about Chicago is vulgar and degrading!). Thus I paid little attention to them. However, Fosse was a choreographer. One must permit the storyteller his craft. In fact, the hospital dance sequences are brilliant and deeply moving. They prepare us for the death of man who has squandered everything, perhaps even a chance at God's love.

The final number is in the form of a roast presided over by Ben Vereen who depicts Joe Gideon as a selfish, driven man who never had any time for life and love and "all that jazz." Joe sings his goodbye to "happiness and sweet caress" before an audience of the important people in his life. Only his daughter Michelle seems sad at his announcement "I think I'm going to die!" Michelle and Angelique who is lurking at the door of the theater where the roast is occurring.

Joe runs down the aisle, shaking hands or kissing his goodbyes. Then suddenly he is walking down the long corridor, a broad smile of expectation and joy on his face. At the end of the corridor in all her bridal finery, Angelique waits for him.

A final cut to the hospital morgue where someone zips up a plastic body bag as the chorus cynically sings, "There's no business like show business!"

Those are the final options Bob Fosse seems to be telling us—the warm marriage bed with the fair spouse or the cold slab in the morgue. We must make our choice about which we will believe to be the truth.

Fosse died several years later of his final heart attack. Nobody, as far as I know, every asked him about what the film meant. I could find no evidence that, like most of those who have been through an NDE, he was never again afraid of death. Nor is there anything on the record to indicate that he was looking forward to meeting once again the Fair Bride of whom Ms. Lange was the image and likeness.

God a passionate and romantic lover? Why not? A sexy woman as a metaphor for God's love? Why not, unless women are inferior to men as sacraments.

Does God really love us that much?

Should there be a God, would it not be necessary that She love us that much and even more?

Would any God who was less attractive and less attracted than Jessica Lange in *All That Jazz* not be the real God at all?

The Irish priest and poet, Paul Murray, a man as unlike Bob Fosse as anyone could possibly be, describes the same kind love:

> He who gives all the gifts we bring
> He who needs nothing,
> Has need for us.
> If you and I should cease to exist,
> He would die of sadness.

A.M.G.

5

Babette's Feast of Love:
Symbols Subtle but Patent

Metaphors are strange realities. Sometimes the implied comparison is so complex that one must examine it, ponder it, wrestle with it, and only after long contemplation understand what it means—for example the happy death imagery in the novel and film by William Kennedy, *Ironweed,* or the forgiveness theme in *Flatliners.* At other times, a rich, powerful, and deeply moving metaphor is immediately transparent. Neither kind of metaphor is inherently better than the other, neither kind implies greater skill on the part of the artist who created it. There is however a special kind of admirable delicacy about the metaphor which in effect dazzles one immediately and thoroughly.

When one is dealing with college students who think they know everything and have instant, if not always well-reasoned, opinions, one can never be sure how they will react. Before the fact, I suspected that they would miss the Eucharistic imagery in the wondrous 1987 Danish film (directed by Gabriel Axel) *Babette's Feast (Babettes Gaestebud).* They had vigorously questioned my contention that Jessica Lange and Audrey Hepburn were metaphors for God. How could they possibly see Babette (Stephane Audran) as a Christ figure? They did "get it," however, immediately and unanimously. On subsequent reflection I realized that the imagery of the Eucharist (or Holy Communion or The Lord's Supper) is still powerful in most Christian denominations. The young people knew a feast of love when they saw it. Isak Dinesen (Karen von Blixen, Meryl Streep in the film *Out of Africa*) wrote the story about a feast of love which was implicitly Eucharistic and Axel faithfully adapted it into a film. God was in the movie so subtly that you could barely see Her. Yet in the end you would have to be blind to miss Her. Both the novella and the film were high art indeed, that simple kind of high art which one never forgets. The film is one of the very best stories of God in the movies—and one of the most powerful because it shocks and dazzles us with its suggestion that God is not only a God of love but a God of self-sacrificing love, a God like Jesus and like Babette.

This delicately told and moving story is about the two devout daughters (Martine and Philippa) of a pietistic and extremely conservative Danish Lutheran minister and their French servant who represents a very different kind of Christianity (French Catholicism) which, however, is somehow not inconsistent with that of the pastor. The story is set in a small, remote, austere Jutland seaside town in the mid-nineteenth century, a setting much like that of Dreyer's film *Ordet*. Compared to Jutland, the Michigan Dunes in the middle of winter look like Pago Pago. After the Pastor's death, the daughters devote their lives to continuing the work of their father in service of God, and in care for their needy townspeople. They hold together a tiny community of survivors of the Pastor's congregation, a community which as it grows older becomes increasingly difficult and contentious. Philippa had turned down a promising opera career—and the love of her French voice coach (a famous opera singer himself)—to remain with her father and the town. Martine had rejected the suit of a promising young military officer. The viewer of the film laments that these lovely young women have turned their backs on marriage and love to serve what seems to be both a lost and an unattractive cause. What a waste it seems.

Many years later the French singer sends a woman (Babette)—who had lost her family in an outbreak of civil war to live with the sisters. They have no money to pay her. So traumatized has she been by the revolution in France and by the death of her family that she offers to work for only her food and a place to sleep. Soon the aging women become dependent on her loyalty and affection. She turns out to be an excellent cook, housekeeper, and a shrewd shopper. The daughters love her because she is so good to them. She loves them perhaps because they have become a substitute family.

Then God's grace intervenes in a typically unexpected way. Babette wins the lottery. The aging women are brokenhearted. She will leave them and return to France. What will they do without her? Before she leaves, however, she will prepare a feast as a memorial to the Pastor's

100th birthday. The members of the little congregation, accustomed to Babette's meals, become skeptical about the elaborate plans. Obviously it will be too much, too sensual, too pleasurable, to grand. They want the Pastor's daughters to stop Babette. However, they love her too much to do that. They will eat the meal but will not enjoy it. To be true to their father's disapproval they remove his picture from the dining room.

The congregation comes to the feast, aging, churlish, quarrelsome, disapproval on their stern and unsmiling faces. The twelfth guest is the officer who once courted Martine. Now a successful general and part of the Establishment he has come to impress the woman with what she lost when she rejected him.

That there are twelve at the table is the first strong hint that the feast will become a Eucharist, enough to tell us what the story is really about. Gabriel Axel found the symbol in Isak Dinesen's story and integrated it into the film (as he did the precise menu for the feast).

The glittering crystal and china, the many courses of wine and food[1] melt the hearts of everyone. Anger, resentment, grudges melt away. Babette triumphs. The General announces that there is only one woman in the world who could create such a festival, a chef so gifted that her meals were called "a love affair of the noble and romantic . . . in which one no longer distinguished between bodily and spiritual appetite." He then speaks of grace of God which transcends time and space and quotes the Pastor's favorite psalm, "Righteousness and bliss have kissed one another." Whether the meal would have in fact melted the heart of the old clergyman too is perhaps open to question. Yet there is so much warmth and love in the room that one is tempted to think that he too would have been won over. The company moves outside to sing and dance under the stars. The general tells Martine that they have never been separated, that in God's grace they have always been together.

Both Dinesen and Axel are alluding to one of the most consoling passages in the Bible—Isaiah 25,6-9:

> Here on Mount Zion the lord Almighty will prepare a banquet for all the nations of the world, a banquet of the richest food and the finest wine. Here he will suddenly remove the cloud of sorry that has been hanging over all the nations. The Sovereign Lord will destroy death forever! He will wipe away the tears from everyone's eyes and take away the disgrace his people suffered throughout the world. The Lord himself has spoken. When it happens, everyone will say, "he is our God! We have put our trust in him and now we are happy and joyful because he has saved us."

The guests depart. The daughters lament that Babette will now return to Paris. She assures them that she will not and cannot. She has spent all the lottery money on the feast. She will remain with them for the rest of their lives.

Babette's self-sacrificing love marks her as Christ figure. Her festival of love, her Eucharist which dissolves time and space and anger and resentment is a memorial of the last supper. It is the Mass, Holy Communion, the Lord's Supper. Babette has become a metaphor for Jesus as the banquet host at the festival of creation and redemption.

Babette, as Edward McNulty puts it (*Christianity and the Arts,* Spring 1991), "gives everything she has to deliver a group of people from their spare, colorless and loveless religion. She invites those who have chosen meagerness to a feast, to taste with joy of the abundance of life. She transforms a little gathering of ascetics into an affair of beauty and splendor. As an image of Christ the Lover, she has wooed them out of darkness into the light of God's presence."

She has done that indeed. However, she has not demeaned the old Pastor's religion. Rather she has built on it and integrated it into a broader worldview, one in which asceticism and splendor are not necessarily opposed to one another. Righteousness and bliss do kiss. Love annuls time and space. At the center of Dinesen's story is the insight that self-sacrificing love redeems everyone and everything. Not only is grace everywhere, but everything *is* grace.

Babette represents God's self-sacrificing love without any appeal to the supernatural events of *All That Jazz* or *Always.* Axel, relying on Dinesen's luminous story, does not have to appeal to special divine interventions. We do not need either Hap or Angelique breaking into the human condition to work their wonders. We need only the story of a family meal that recreates love, the sort of event that happens every day and yet on some special days becomes transformative because of the sacrifices of the cook. God fills the room yet is quite invisible. Grace is everywhere but discrete and unobtrusive, as it normally (always?) is in our lives. Unhesitatingly we say, yes of course this is a family meal and this is the Last Supper and the Lord's Supper and we know exactly what the story is about. Both the novella and the film are works of religious genius, though there is no evidence that either Axel or Dinesen were deeply religious people.

As much as I like *All That Jazz,* and *Always,* and *Breaking the Waves,* and the God figures represented by Jessica Lange, and Audrey Hepburn, and Emily Watson, I must admit that from the point of view of artistic genius and theological power *Babette's Feast* is superior to them. No one has to point out to an audience that Stephane Audran is a Christ figure. No one has to say this story is about the transformative power of self-sacrificing love. The story, both enchanting and ordinary, says it all without any need of exegesis.

Time and space need never stand in the way of love.

And as Babette tells Martine and Phillipa, an artist is never poor.

Note

1. Our colleague and friend Michael Hout, a skilled cook among his many other talents, once prepared Babette's Feast for the liturgy committee in his parish. He did not, however, kill a turtle for the turtle soup!

A.M.G.

6

Is This Heaven? No, It's Iowa

Field of Dreams, a 1989 movie starring Kevin Costner seems some-what simple on the surface—an homage to baseball and father-son re-lationships. But upon a moment's reflection, it is much more complex. With dead ballplayers coming back to life, a mysterious disembodied Voice talking to someone in a cornfield, and a time warp that transports the lead character back in time as he steps out of a motel room, this movie is anything but obvious. Ray Kinsella (Kevin Costner), like his deceased father John Kinsella, loves baseball which is warmly portrayed with images of stadiums (Fenway Park), players (Shoeless Joe Jack-son), old uniforms (1919 White Sox), and lots of pitching, hitting, slid-ing, and the ever present jocular banter between players. Such an ideal-ized portrayal of baseball has long been a metaphor for American life, and when it appears in such a mystical film we are clearly being asked to suspend judgment and enter into a world promising to be rich in symbolism.

In the Garden of Eden

The movie opens by panning to the blue sky where a shaft of light beams down on Iowa cornfields—perhaps a hint of God's presence? Everything is still and quiet; it feels primal and virginal, with an Old Testament feel about it. Where Adam was in the Garden of Eden, Ray Kinsella is in his cornfield; where the voice of God speaks to Adam, a low, firm, commanding voice now speaks to Ray, "*If you build it, he will come*." Who is this voice and what is it supposed to mean? None of this is made clear, but it doesn't seem to be Ray talking to himself. You believe it's a real voice out there, somewhere. Is it meant to be the voice of God? Who knows. But, prior to each time the voice speaks the camera pans to bright light in the sky, as in the opening scene. Later at night there is a flash of lightning just before the Voice speaks to Ray laying awake in his bed, and again, the next day, we see the sunlight breaking out behind some clouds just before the Voice speaks again. Bright light in the sky is a common metaphor for God's presence and it doesn't seem an accident that this is shown to us immediately before the mysterious Voice speaks.

The command from above to build something out of place with the immediate environment recalls the story of Noah, where God commanded Noah to build an ark. Here the mysterious Voice speaks and Ray takes it as a personal message commanding him to build something: *"If you build it he will come."* At first Ray doesn't know what he is to build, but later is provided a vision when he sees a baseball field in the middle of his corn that includes the 1919 White Sox player Shoeless Joe Jackson. Now he knows he has to build a baseball field right in the middle of the corn like Noah building an ark in the middle of the desert.

But Ray goes ahead—on something like faith—and builds the field. I say faith because there doesn't seem to be any other reason to do this, except that he feels he should. He is, in effect, taking the word of the Voice and if it is meant to be a hint of God, then God is certainly testing Ray's faith, as he is surrounded by doubters and financial difficulty, including his wife ("we used up all our savings on that field, Ray!"); her brother ("How could you plow under your major crop?"); the neighbors ("What the hell is he doing"; "Damn fool"; "He's going to lose his farm"; "Well your husband plowed under his corn and built a baseball field....the weirdo....at least I am not married to the biggest horse's-ass in three counties"). Noah must have been surrounded by similar doubters, building his boat in a desert. There are many interpretations of the story of Noah, of course, but one that seems relevant here is the lesson learned from God's point of view, which is even if I make a mistake, a terrible mistake—and God felt his creation was a mistake and so destroyed it—there is the possibility of starting again. No mistake is final for there is always the possibility of a new beginning. In *Field of Dreams* there is a similar idea, except here it is that death isn't the end, that the mistakes of our life are not final and there is both forgiveness and a chance to start again, seen in the spirits of deceased ball players who are given a chance to play once again on the field that Ray builds. The central player, Shoeless Joe Jackson was banned from baseball for being involved in a scandal to fix the World Series, and what his chance to play ball again on Ray's field seems to be saying is that whatever the fault, crime, sin, or misjudgment of our lives they will not go unforgiven forever.

On Faith

Having built his field Ray now waits alone without a sign or hint that he has done the right thing or is on the right path. He is given no encouragement. He shoulders the burden of his decision alone. He is the lone individual living by his faith (in the Voice) and his faith alone. With a certain degree of angst and uncertainty he wonders what to do next. He just waits. A year passes and nothing happens. Then one evening Ray's daughter Karen tells him that there's a man out there in the baseball field and it turns out it's the 1919 White Sox player Shoeless Joe Jackson.

Karen: "Are you a ghost?"

Shoeless Joe: "What do you think?"

Karen: "You look real to me"

Shoeless Joe: "Then I guess I am real"

Shoeless Joe: "Can I come back again?"

Ray: "Yes, I built this for you"

Shoeless Joe: "Is this Heaven?"

Ray: "No, its Iowa"

"*Is this heaven?*" Shoeless Joe asks, and Ray tells him: "*No, it's Iowa.*" But when you think about it this baseball field doesn't look like just Iowa, for we often see it at night glowing in the illumination of stadium lights and it appears quite heavenly. Further, when Shoeless Joe first appears his white uniform is lit by these same stadium lights such that he literally glows against the dark green infield grass, shimmering like some kind of ghost or spirit being. At other times, the stadium lights reflect off what must be low-lying fog creating what appears to be white clouds above the baseball field, as if the field is floating in the sky. Shoeless Joe seems to realize that he is getting a chance to play baseball again, and with the game as a metaphor for life, he is getting a chance to live again. This suggests he has, in fact, arrived in heaven. And from what we see out there in the movie house audience —that glowing island in the sky of a baseball field which somehow attracts deceased souls—we too know it is meant to be heaven. The game meant everything to these players. It was their life, it was all they lived for and cared about, and their playing careers were all abruptly interrupted. As Shoeless Joe said, "Getting thrown out of baseball was like getting part of me amputated." And now, after death, he finds himself in a beautiful baseball park somewhere in his afterlife. It acts like heaven too, for Ray pitches to Shoeless Joe and he gets to hit some home runs, and if part of Joe was amputated, he is now made whole.

He must be in Heaven. Where else could he be? But if that's the case, why does Ray tell him, "No, it's Iowa." Why aren't these wandering souls ever told, "yes, this is heaven, you have arrived; welcome." What further complicates this story is that these players aren't even sure themselves where they are. Here is this "heavenly" baseball field glowing in the dark and seemingly floating in the sky, and here are these ghosts of deceased players getting a chance at baseball (life) after death. How could any of them not know they are in some place like Heaven? But, that's the amazing thing: they don't know where they are. They're babes in the woods. They just stand there in complete amazement, and ask, "Is this heaven?" only to be told "No, its Iowa." It looks like heaven (to a ballplayer), it feels like heaven (their dreams have come true, they are playing baseball again, they are living again), they can't believe it isn't heaven. They just look around as if to say, "Iowa....Iowa, how can I, I mean why does my spirit, end up in, in, Iowa? This has got to be heaven. I will ask again, is this Heaven?" And again they are told, "No, its Iowa."

What then does this say about the religious imagination? This denial of what everyone knows to be the case—that this is, in fact, heaven— reflects a more transcendent, or Protestant-like religious imagination, where there is no trace of God's presence in the created world. To tell the truth to these poor wondering souls that they had, in fact, arrived in Heaven, makes immanent and viscerally present what is believed to be transcendent. In a sense Shoeless Joe is asking for a sign, a hint, a suggestion, that heavenly salvation is possible, that there is life after death. "No, this is Iowa," is a constant reaffirmation of a cold, hard reality untouched by grace experiences. It is also a lonely reality that is drama-

tized in the isolation and anxiety that accompanies Ray's faith (building that field). That baseball field is a hint of a heavenly presence; but
in a religious imagination for which God exists only in transcendent
form there is no room for such hints of a divine presence.

Ingmar Bergman in Iowa

In this worldview one could imagine these poor souls wandering for
fifty, a hundred, a thousand years, and each time they ask, "Is this
Heaven?" they will be told, "No, it's Iowa; no it's this; no it's that; no,
no, no." In the dispirited look on Shoeless Joe's face when Ray tells
him he is not in heaven we can see the deep loneliness of the classic
Protestant worldview devoid of sacramental hints of God's presence. I
had always thought that the bleak Nordic lives portrayed in Ingmar
Bergman films constituted the quintessential cinematic expression of
austere Protestantism, where characters are thrown back upon themselves to wonder and search, in a state of constant agitation, over the
meaning of their faith. *Field of Dreams* is not usually seen as part of
this tradition at all. It is usually described either positively, as says the
video jacket, "a heartwarming experience.....a glowing tribute to all who
dare to dream," or negatively as a corny, maudlin American movie. It is
rarely thought of in Bergman-like terms as a treatise on austere Protestantism, but there is a harshness of judgment in the "No, it's Iowa"
refrain, and a certain sort of self-tortured anxiety about Ray and his
personal private decision to stick by his faith in the Voice. He is not
deeply troubled, agreed, but one of characters he meets (Terrence Mann
played by James Earl Jones) thinks he is something of a nut case with
all his talk about voices and personal visions, and his mother and brother-
in-law both feel he is blinded by this rigid adherence to building this
baseball field in the middle of the family farm.

The Two Imaginations

For a comparison with a more immanent religious imagination, consider *Jacob's Ladder*, where at movie's end Vietnam vet Jacob Singer
is dying in his home. He walks over to a staircase that will symbolically
take his soul up to Heaven, and sees his young son (who died earlier)
sitting on the bottom step, something of an angel to accompany him up
the ladder to Heaven. Jacob is surprised, and calls out his son's name,

who then turns his head toward his father and says assuredly, "It's OK...come on, let's go up." Jacob now walks toward the staircase and his son reaches out his hand, and together, the son leading, they ascend the staircase into a sea of bright light which engulfs them when they reach the top. Here is a different religious imagination, where there is not only the hint of an afterlife (the white light), a way to get there (the staircase), but also an angelic guide to accompany the ascent to Heaven (Jacob's deceased son). Comfort, care, guidance, and direction, all hints of God's loving presence made manifest to Jacob Singer at the end of his life. At the top of the stairs, surrounded by white light, he does not ask, "Is this Heaven?"

Imagine this same scene done in the religious imagination of *Field of Dreams*. If Jacob, say, were to ask, "Is this the ladder to Heaven?", his son might reply, "No, its just the staircase in our house," or "Is this enveloping white light heaven?" he would be told, "No, its just the hall light bulb." Consider another example, *All That Jazz*, where the metaphoric representation of God, or an angel of God, is not a distant disembodied male voice but a sensuous, beautiful woman, like Jessica Lange. She doesn't command or expect obedience as a matter of faith. Rather, she comforts, cajoles, and flirts with Joe Gideon (Roy Scheider) as he approaches his death. And, like the Tim Robbins character in *Jacob's Ladder*, when he dies he does not go alone. Jessica Lange, perhaps an angel of death, is there to lovingly accompany him down a long corridor to what must be Heaven's door. Imagine Shoeless Joe appearing in *All That Jazz*, on the operating table like Joe Gideon, inquiring as to whether this was a precursor to ascending to heaven. Would the angelic figure of Jessica Lange say, "No, this is just an illusion induced by the anesthesia you are taking." Or, if Ray Kinsella were in *All That Jazz* and was asked about Heaven, I think he might have said, "Yes, I think this is Heaven." I don't think he would have said, "No, its Iowa."

In *Field of Dreams* and *All That Jazz* Ray Kinsella and Joe Gideon worry and regret many of their life's decisions—Ray's troubled relation with his dad; Joe's complex relations with his ex-wife, daughter, and present lover. Ray's struggles seem mostly with himself; he was commanded to build this damned field, commanded to travel to meet strangers for reasons he didn't understand, and wondered, all through the movie, what was the reason for doing all this. Joe Gideon also had problems in his life, and he talked about them, but mostly to the Angel Jessica Lange, who cajoled, forgave, teased, and engaged in a playful exchange with Joe's troubled soul. She responded to his confessions of failure in love, marriage, fidelity, and substance abuse, with understanding and forgiveness. More generally, *All That Jazz* presents a very sensuous universe, filled with the pungent smells, colors, and a complete range of human strengths and failings. In art historical terms it is a very Baroque cinematic canvas, as in the work of Caravaggio, Rubens, or Frans Hals, *Field of Dreams* is Realism, rendered more in the manner of Dürer, Vermeer, or Edward Hopper.

These two movies, then, are examples of the opposite ends of the religious imagination spectrum. One is David Tracy's analogic imagination, wherein God and Heaven are imagined as being like this or that human attribute, so that God's loving embrace is like that of a sensual and sexy woman and God's love awaits all of us like a lover awaits, sweet, tender, caring, forgiving. God's love, then, is like Jessica Lange's love for Joe Gideon. *All That Jazz* is the analogic imagination at its best. At the other end of the spectrum lies a film like *Field of Dreams*, Tracy's dialogic imagination, where God and Heaven are imagined as being not like this or that human attribute, so that Heaven is not like a baseball field. It is a great simplification, but the differences between the analogic and dialogic imaginations are nowhere better seen than in the idea that God is like a beautiful woman and Heaven is not like a baseball field.

If Ray is best described as driven by his inner vision (to build the field) and commanded from the outside by this cosmic Voice toward a sense of Heaven, then Joe Gideon is best described as being pulled toward Heaven by the loving hints of Jessica Lange's Angelique character. If Ray is more the man of personal integrity and honesty; one to keep his word and to keep the faith, then Joe is more the man of human failings, lack of discipline, too many broken promises, and too many drugs. Ray and Joe are the two sides of all of us and in their responses the two sides of the religious imagination. Joe is all of our failings rolled up into one man's life, and Jessica Lange, as the angel Angelique, is ultimate love and forgiveness rolled up into one woman's sensual presence, suggests *All That Jazz*. Ray is our tenacity of belief, the strength of faith, the human tendency to want to believe, even without evidence, hints, or concrete reasons why. Ray's meeting his long deceased father is his redemption of that belief, and the suggestion of the possibility of a Heaven. As Ray says at movie's end, *"Maybe this is Heaven."* *Field of Dreams* suggests our willingness to believe, even if the world offers us no signs or comfort. These movies are contrasting pictures of a cosmos where God is built into the world she created and one where she is above, beyond, and outside her created world.

On Redemption

If baseball is a metaphor for life, then the possibility of a game after death is the possibility of life after death, where mistakes and sins—such as those of the 1919 White Sox being banned from baseball—are ultimately forgiven. This is shown in the movie where each character has something go wrong with baseball (their life), and each has it put right when they get to play ball after death. Shoeless Joe was banned for having possibly participated in the fixing of the 1919 World Series. But when his spirit gets to play ball again it's as if the ban has been lifted; to be allowed to play again is, metaphorically, to be forgiven.

Then there is "Moonlight" Graham. Part way into the movie Ray hears the voice again, this time telling him to "Ease his pain." Once again he doesn't know what he is being commanded to do, but at a school meeting over banning the books of the controversial 1960s novelist Terrence Mann, Ray gets the idea that he must find Mann and take him to a ball game at Fenway Park. At the game Ray is given another vision: he sees old-time player Moonlight Graham's name on the scoreboard. Again, he doesn't know what it means or what he is supposed to do, but later Terrence Mann says he heard the Voice too and it said, "Go the distance," which Mann felt meant go the distance to find Moonlight Graham in his hometown of Chisholm, Minnesota. Terrence doesn't know why he should do this, but he too decides to follow the Voice and rides along in Ray's VW bus to Minnesota. It turns out Graham had quit baseball and become a doctor. Further, Doc Graham, as he is now called, has been dead for years. Ray and Terrence don't know what to do, but as Ray steps out of a motel he finds himself in a time warp. He's back in 1972 and encounters the then living "Doc" Graham walking down the street. They talk:

Ray: "If you could do anything you wanted."

Doc: "Are you the kind of man who could grant me that wish?"

Ray: "I don't know, I am just asking."

Doc: "I never got to bat in the big leagues...that's what I wish."

Doc: "Is there enough magic out there in the moonlight to make this dream come true?"

Ray: "What would you say if I said yes."

Doc: "I'd believe you."

Ray: "There's a place where things like that happen and if you want to go I can take you."

Doc, though, decides to stay in Minnesota so Ray and Terrence drive back to Iowa. On the way home they pick up a young hitchhiker who surprises them by introducing himself as Archie Graham. They look at each other and then realize this is the young Doc Graham just starting his baseball career. Archie rides back to Iowa and joins the many other ghost players who have come to play on Ray's field. Doc (as Archie) finally gets to bat and actually drives in a run.

What was missing in his life has just been provided and his soul should now be at peace. It appears that it is. This is beautifully visualized when Ray and Annie's daughter Karen slips and falls from the bleachers while watching the game. She appears seriously hurt and Annie runs to call a doctor. Kneeling by her, Ray looks up and sees the young Archie Graham walking toward them. He reaches the white pebbles that border the field, momentarily stops, looks down, drops his glove, and as he steps across the rock line he turns into the older Doc Graham. He diagnoses Karen as choking and slaps her on the back dislodging a piece of hot dog. Having left the field he now knows he can't go back to being the young Archie Graham, and while Ray is upset about this, there is a deep acceptance and serenity on Doc Graham's face. He has had his time at bat, he accomplished what he couldn't in life, and now he too is ready to walk out into center field and disappear into the corn stalks. He walks past the other players who have stopped playing and are watching him. They congratulate him on how good he played as his younger self, Archie Graham. "*You were good, rookie*" says Shoeless Joe. When he reaches the cornstalks, that border center field he stops, looks back, and then disappears into the corn. A beautiful metaphor for ascending to heaven and being finally at peace, being allowed to do in an afterlife what one had missed when alive.

The next to find peace is Terrence Mann, the ornery, cynical, and cranky old novelist Ray finds in Boston who follows him back to Iowa to see Ray's baseball field. The next day Shoeless Joe asks Terrence if he wants to come and join the other players. Terrence thinks for a moment and says yes, he wants to join the others on the field of dreams. Terrence isn't a spirit like the others, but it turns out that he too had aspirations about baseball that were not fulfilled. He tells Ray that he had always wanted to play with Jackie Robinson on the Brooklyn Dodgers but never got a chance because they tore down Ebbets Field. Like Shoeless Joe and Doc it is now Terrence Mann's time to get his second chance and realize what he couldn't during his lifetime. With this chance he seems a changed man. When we first met him he was very difficult. He didn't want to meet Ray, didn't want to talk about the meaning of the 1960s, didn't want to go to Fenway Park, and felt the talk of visions and voices made Ray a borderline mental case. Now, though, walking toward these cornstalks in center field he has a grin that is a mile wide and giggles like a child as he sticks his finger into the cornstalks to see what's really out there. He is no longer the ornery, cynical, cranky novelist. He turns back for a last look and then, smiling, he walks into the cornfield and disappears. Like Doc's going, Terrence's is peaceful and full of joy.

The Protestant Ethic and the Spirit of Baseball

All That Jazz's Joe Gideon faces a good many of real-life problems and uncertainties—will he be able to maintain his relationship with his girlfriend, will his substance abuse problems get worse, how will his relationship with his ex-wife work out, will he get his Broadway dance musical and edit his movie on schedule, and most importantly, since he has had a heart attack, will he live or die? His is a world of uncertainties, crises, and pressure, all the preconditions that should create an anxiety-ridden personality and spiritual questioning: what is the meaning of my life, why am I dying, what is the purpose of existence, and so forth. It's not that Joe Gideon is incapable of these questions, they just don't seem to come up. He does think about his life, its failures, his weaknesses and shortcomings as a man, husband, and father, but it is surprisingly free of larger cosmic import. He mostly sits and talks with the metaphoric angel of death, Jessica Lange, confessing and reminiscing about his shortcomings. She doesn't get too upset either. She listens, laughs, cajoles, and humors him, saying, in effect, yes, Joe you did this and that, but you are still a good person. Their relationship is all very sweet and loving. In this sense there is very little mental angst in this movie.

Compare this with *Field of Dream's* Ray Kinsella. He is almost the opposite. His life is in bucolic Iowa, on a small farm, with a loving wife, wonderful daughter, friendly neighbors, and considering the turbulent 1960s of his past, he is living some sort of pastoral dream. If Joe Gideon has a turbulent life but a relatively calm spiritual existence, Ray has a calm life but a very anxiety-ridden spiritual life. He is visited by visions, mysterious voices, a belief no one else seems to hold, and an inability to let go of his visions. To say he is tortured is too strong, but he is certainly conflicted, anxious, alone, and in constant ferment over what he is supposed to do. It is an interesting mix of uncertainty and being driven. He lies in bed at night and tells Annie of his anguish over what he has, and hasn't made of his life, and then there are the cosmic voices and visions. Nothing is clear to him.

At the root of Ray Kinsella's angst lies a deep uncertainty over what he has been asked to do by a distant, omnipotent, cosmic power (what else could that deep rumbling Voice be). Ray is riddled with metaphysical uncertainty. He isn't sure why the Voice contacted him ("What do you want from me!") or what the Voice meant by, "If you build it, he will come," and once he figures that out he isn't clear why he did what he did ("I just completed something totally illogical, am I totally nuts?") or, finally, having built that baseball field, having seen all those ghost players arrive, and having almost lost his farm to the bank, he still has no idea what all this meant for him ("What's in it for me!").

But the uncertainty is tied to his self-disciplined and largely ascetic behavior. His beliefs—in the omnipotent Voice and the uncertainty of its ultimate plan for his life—give his personality a motivational dynamic that drives him onward in a systematic, rational, ascetic pursuit of his goals. For no financial, political, social, literary, or any other reason, he builds that baseball field. For no particular reason other than his belief in the Voice he drives to Boston to meet a perfect stranger, the novelist T. Mann. Then, for no reason except another vision and voice, he drives on to Minnesota to look for Doc Graham. The point here is that this is not instrumental behavior. This is not economically motivated behavior derived from a calculation of costs and benefits. This is a moral stance, an ethic, with characteristics like asceticism, self-discipline, and self-mastery, which sounds exactly like the personality type identified by the great German sociologist Max Weber in his famous essay on *The Protestant Ethic and the Spirit of Capitalism.* For Weber this was the cultural underpinning of our modern commercial civilization, and it seems also manifest here too. Ray Kinsella would seem to have a goodly amount of the Protestant Ethic as classically identified by Weber. It doesn't lead to capital accumulation, at least as far as we know, but it is reflective of a religious orientation associated with the rise of modernity.

And it appears as a religious ethic, for with all the tranquility of his life, what intrudes is a question of spirit and faith, of trying to understand the purposes behind an omnipotent being (that Voice) that isn't clear about what it wants from you. For Weber it was that uncertainty in the Protestant worldview that created the anxiety resulting in disciplined ascetic behavior. For Ray it is the uncertainty about what the Voice has specifically in mind that generates Ray's anxiety and his disciplined behavior to constantly do what he feels he must to try and figure out what the Voice means and what it has in store for him. For Weber's Protestants this is not known until death, and so the uncertainty and resultant dynamism of personality is a constant throughout life. The same seems true for Ray. He doesn't know what is in store for him throughout the movie and spends his life in his ascetic and self-disciplined way trying to figure it all out. If the Protestant worldview is that you just don't know, that is certainly the case with Ray. He never knows until the movie's end.

There is another aspect of Weber's Protestant Ethic that centers more on work being an almost religious calling, not merely an instrumental activity. In the movies *Always* and *Ghost* the reason the wandering souls could not find peace was an inability to let go of loved ones here on earth. Once that was resolved they were freed and could seemingly take their places in an eternal heavenly peace. What do they need resolved? It's not attachment to loved ones, nor do they need some kind of absolution for having lied, cheated, or for any other human failing. No, their spiritual disquiet has to do with job and career. What had happened to all of them was that their baseball careers were unexpectedly interrupted, so what heaven means isn't so much reuniting with lost loved ones, or even making it to the World Series, being a twenty-game pitcher, winning the home run title, or any other prize. All they wanted was to play the game. Mostly this has been commented upon as this movie's homage to the glories of the American pastime, and it certainly does that. But what's interesting is to note the sense of the Weberian Protestant Ethic in all of them, baseball as a calling. Shoeless Joe says he would have played for just the food money, he loved the game so much. And Doc Graham, when Ray asks him if he could do anything he wanted what does he answer, "I never got to bat in the big leagues...that's what I wish." What was interrupted was their careers. That's what they yearn for, that's what's incomplete, and that's what the field of dreams, Heaven, can make whole again: careers. Work. Not the ends of work. It isn't religious practices (baseball here) for only instrumental reasons, but for themselves, as baseball for the sake of baseball is work for the sense of work, is, following Weber, an ascetic religious practice for the sake of a religious ascetic practice. Because God's wishes and desires are unknowable, because for Calvin it is impossible to know if God has chosen you as one of the elect, all you can do, all you should do, is engage in self-disciplined ascetic behavior, like monastic religious practices now writ large: religious practices, work practices, baseball practices, all sacred. It was work and career that was interrupted, and most importantly it was work and career that was made whole again in Heaven when they all got to play ball again. There was a time when work and career were separate from religious practice, but the idea of the sacred nature of work changed all that to a large degree. Now it is not only not profane, but something that is legitimately healed in Heaven. In our world where careers are how we define ourselves and count our major contributions, not only instrumentally but morally, a premature interruption of that career is something the modern religious imagination would conceive of being made whole once again in Heaven.

Ray's Walk of Faith

Finally, we come to the fate of Ray Kinsella and the reason he built the baseball field in the first place. Ray is the last of the major characters to find out the meaning of his having built the field. On the surface it has to do with his relationship to his deceased father. Driving the VW bus back to Iowa after visiting Doc Graham in Minnesota, Ray talks to Terrence about his dad and how he didn't make it as a baseball player but always tried to get his son into the game. Ray refused to play and in anger told his dad he would never play catch with him again. And if that wasn't enough he also told him he couldn't respect a man whose hero was a criminal, meaning Shoeless Joe. Ray would later leave home and his dad would die so he never got a chance to apologize. "Son of a bitch died before I could take it back, before I could tell him." Remorsefully, driving along on a lonely road at night, talking to Terrence, Ray now wishes somehow he could make it all right, take it all back, tell his dad he didn't mean what he said, and let his dad meet his wife Annie and their daughter Karen. Terrence just listens and comes to the personal conclusion that building this field was Ray's penance. Ray couldn't bring back his dad, so he brought back his dad's hero Shoeless Joe. Ray doesn't disagree. None of this has made any sense to him throughout the whole movie and this seems as good an explanation as any. Ever since the opening scene when the Voice commands, Ray has been operating in the dark.

Their Volkswagen bus rolls on through the night, and as they approach home you see that baseball field glowing in the dark lit by stadium lights. It looks otherworldly; there is no doubt about it, it looks like Heaven. The next day Ray looks at Shoeless Joe and says, "What are you grinning at, you ghost?" Knowingly, Shoeless Joe replies, "If you build it [turns his head toward someone over there] he will come." Ray says "it was you," and Shoeless Joe replies, "No, it was you." Ray then turns his eyes where Shoeless Joe is looking and sees a young man putting on a catcher's equipment. The camera zooms in closer and Ray knows it's his dad as a much younger man. It's John Kinsella, like Archie Graham, just starting out in baseball, well before Ray had entered his life. Ray had built the field out of faith, and now that faith is being redeemed as he is united with his father. They can now repair all that death had interrupted. Once again the old refrain, *"Is this heaven,"* but now, at movie's end, the answer is a little different.

John Kinsella: "Its so beautiful here, its like a dream come true....Is this Heaven?"

Ray Kinsella: "It's Iowa."

John Kinsella: "I could have sworn it was Heaven."

Ray Kinsella: "Is there a Heaven?"

John Kinsella: "Oh, yea, its the place where dreams come true."

Ray Kinsella: "Maybe this is Heaven."

"Maybe this is Heaven," says Ray. At last, at movie's end, some acknowledgment of what by now we all know to be true: this field of dreams is, in fact, Heaven, and now Ray, like Shoeless Joe, Doc Graham, and Terrence Mann can do all the things his father's death had interrupted. He wanted his dad to meet his family, and so now he introduces his father to his wife Annie and daughter Karen. They go into the house so father and son can have a little time together. After a while John and Ray shake hands and say goodbye to each other. As John walks back toward the cornfield in center field Ray says, "Hey dad, you wanna have a catch?" John replies, "I'd like that." And then in a scene that never fails to bring a huge surge of emotion to all who watch, and particularly for fathers and sons, they play catch. In what must be the mother of all metaphors for father and son bonding they play a simple game of catch, and in that baseball going back and forth connecting father and son we feel forgiveness and love. It is a simple, yet powerful metaphor for a connection between the living and the dead, for a sense of the eternity of existence. At the end of *All That Jazz* Joe Gideon walks toward the beautiful Angelique and the hint of their sexual union is a beautiful and loving metaphor, a heavenly embrace at the end of life. In both films it is the same belief that death is not the end, that there is something out there, whether metaphorically expressed as a baseball field or a beautiful woman, it is a positive human affirmation that death does not triumph over life. In saying "Maybe this is Heaven" Ray's journey of faith is now complete. Ray has undergone a transformation too. He came to have faith, overcame doubt, and found that faith redeemed when he met his father.

Afternoon soon turns to evening, and father and son continue to play catch. Annie watches from the porch and then goes inside. They continue to play. It's now night, and they are still throwing. The camera now pulls away and we see the field glimmering in the illumination provided by the stadium lights. It is an island of light in the surrounding darkness, and as the camera pulls further away we see a long string of car lights heading toward this field of dreams. It is a visual answer to the question that has haunted the whole film: "Is this Heaven?" The answer given in this image is yes, and further, it is where people want to go. Just follow the string of headlights; they point to the field of dreams. Then the camera takes one last pan from the field up to the blue sky, an image which is held for a second or two, and then the fade to black. It is now complete, this is where the movie started, the opening shot was of the sky and the hint of God and then down to humans and their fields of corn. Now, at the end, it is from the human condition back up to the hint of God in the sky.

A.J.B.

7

Pale Rider

Not all religious imagery on the silver screen is graceful and sacramental. God is understood to be not only immanent in creation leaving signs of her loving grace, but also above and beyond the world, judging the conduct of mankind. Such a religious imagination can be seen in Clint Eastwood's *Pale Rider* (1985), in which he plays that mysterious stranger, "The Man with No Name," who appears out of nowhere to side with the good and punish the bad.

I was used to this mysterious stranger from earlier Eastwood films, *A Fist Full of Dollars* (1964), *For a Few Dollars More* (1965), and *The Good, the Bad, and the Ugly* (1966). The sensibility of these movies was dominated by the eerie music of Enio Morricone and the dramatic direction of Sergio Leone. His close-ups of sunburned, weathered, and dusty faces, gave these westerns an emotional impact that went far beyond anything their plot structure or actor's skills would lead one to expect. In retrospect the Leone/Morricone low budget western seemed to have been more pure form than any particular content, let alone religious content.

Pale Rider (1985) was in this same mold, without, of course, Sergio Leone's direction and Enio Morricone's music. Like the earlier films, the plot remained minimal: the mysterious stranger once again rides into a western town to protect the deserving and kill the wicked. Here the setting is northern California in 1850, with homesteading miners being driven off their land by a mining company that wants to possess the gold fields where they have settled. Into this situation enters the Clint Eastwood character of no past and no future, the dusty, slightly grizzled lone rider, who sides with the miners giving them the faith to

71

go on, and in the climactic scene, destroying the mining company and its hired hands.

The fact that the "Man with No Name" is not located in any social or institutional space, makes this character something of an empty set, or a signifier awaiting signification. That is, having no identity allows him to be defined any way the film desires. In the earlier films the identity mystery seemed part of the appeal, particularly when combined with Enio Morricone's haunting scores. While there is still a good deal of mystery over exactly who the mysterious stranger is in *Pale Rider* there are also strong hints that he is meant to be something like an avenging angel of God, or the Messiah returning to judge the conduct of mankind at the biblically prophesied judgment day.

Clint Eastwood as Jesus Christ is not a thought that comes easily to anyone's mind, I understand. But this hypothesis is not just a particular interpretation "read into the movie" by a sociologist looking for religious imagination in contemporary film. The religious references and hints are there, to be seen on the screen. *Pale Rider* illustrates that the religious imagination is alive and well, if not downright irrepressible, and can be found in everything from comedies (*Oh, God!, Mr. Destiny, Ground Hog Day*), to romantic comedies (*Truly, Madly, Deeply*), to hokey love stories (*Always*), to serious drama (*Fearless, Jacob's Ladder, Flatliners*), to musicals (*All That Jazz*), to feel-good movies about baseball (*Field of Dreams*) even to westerns (*Pale Rider*).

The religious imagination is actually very active in this movie, and centers upon a Christ-like figure who executes the biblically prophesied last judgment. Michelangelo (1534-41) painted his version of the last judgment as a fresco in the Sistine Chapel and here we have hints of the same biblical prophesy in a 1985 movie. I do not intend a comparison between what to many is a B movie with a great work of Western art, but only wish to make the sociological point that the religious imagination works in multiple media throughout history. Religious representations are not limited to any particular epoch, but seem to recur from fresco to silver screen. To see this more closely we need to turn to the movie itself.

The film opens with a foreboding sense of impending danger: a swarm of riders on horseback thunder across a hillside like a pack of locusts or a dark cloud. You never see the riders' individual faces, only the swarm, going somewhere to do something. The thunder of hooves is loud and we don't know where the riders are going, but there is an ominous feeling that something is about to happen. The film then cuts to a tent camp of peaceful miners, women, children, dogs, a cow. Ordinary God-fearing people going about their daily chores oblivious to an impending attack. Then back to the swarm of riders, the rumble of their hooves like rolling thunder moving across the land. Then back to the miners, who, like animals sensing danger, turn their heads toward the sound of the hooves. With looks of apprehension they sense something is about to happen, and happen it does, as riders pour through the camp, tearing down tents, shooting livestock, and knocking down miners trying to run away. Without a word spoken this opening sequence visually establishes the moral terrain of the story.

In the terror of this raid a teenage girl's little dog is killed, and afterward she walks to a quiet place in the forest to bury her dog and recite the Lord's Prayer. "The Lord is my shepherd, I shall not want—but I do want!" and what she wants is a miracle that will save the community from the clutches of the mining company. She asks for "just one miracle, Amen," and at that point a sunlit hole appears in the clouds and shafts of sunlight stream down upon the land below.

Bright white light like this is a common visual metaphor for God. It appeared in *Fearless,* flickering off an airplane windowpane on Jeff Bridges' face, and also in a "light at the end of the tunnel" metaphor, as a bright light at the open end of his crashed plane's broken fuselage. This was the scene in which Bridges choked on a strawberry and collapsed on his living room floor with his wife trying to revive him. The image of him walking toward the light symbolized his soul leaving his body and going toward heaven. A bright light is also used in *Ghost*. It descends from the heavenly sky to envelope Patrick Swayze and take his soul to heaven.

In *Pale Rider* the stream of light from the heavens appearing right after Megan's prayer for a miracle, seems to signify that God has heard and is somehow answering. That answer comes in the next image where we see, way off in the distance, a lone rider coming toward us. Even closer, we can make out the rider as the Clint Eastwood's "Man with No Name," riding a dapple grey horse. This Pale Rider may very well be metaphoric for an avenging angel sent by God in response to Megan Wheeler's prayers to save the righteous and smite the wicked. Eastwood himself said of the character, "I thought about playing it a little bit like he was sort of an avenging angel."[1] There are clear signs, though, that this mysterious stranger, this "spiritual being or an emissary from a higher plane,"[2] as Eastwood refers to him, may be something besides an avenging angel.

This possibility is hinted at when we look in on Megan Wheeler in her home among the miners. While her mother Sarah (Carrie Snodgrass) is working around the kitchen, Megan is reading from the Bible. She is reading from Revelation: *"And behold a pale horse."* We then see that Eastwood's dapple mount is just such a pale horse. *"And hell followed,"* and looking out her window we see Clint Eastwood, the mysterious stranger, sitting on that pale horse. The full passage from Revelation 6-8:

> I looked, and there before me was a pale horse! Its rider was named Death, and Hades was following close behind him. They were given power over a fourth of the earth to kill by sword...

The miners don't know who he is, and it doesn't seem to matter:

Sarah: *"Who are you, who are you, really!"*

Preacher: *"Really doesn't matter does it?"*

Sarah: *"No"*

He wears a clerical collar, though, and the miners call him "the Preacher." He is certainly meant to signify some religious figure, and given the quotation from Revelation, he would seem to be a metaphor for the Messiah, who has returned for the last judgment. The mysterious stranger gives many hints of being such a Christ-like figure. There is his demeanor, a spiritual stillness and quietness in his presentation of self. He seems to understand situations as if possessing knowledge no one else has. He is always under control, seems to know what he is doing, and demonstrates a Christ-like serenity. He joins Megan, Sarah, and her boyfriend Hull Barrett (Michael Moriarity) for dinner in their small cabin and just stands there in quiet serenity. This slender bearded figure is a common Christ-like image seen before. It is like the master joining his disciples for a meal.

The next day he walks out to where the miners are panning for gold, and in a Christ-like request to disciples humbly asks, "put me to work." Hull tells him there is a boulder sitting in the middle of the creek that can't be broken. The Pale Rider rolls up his sleeves, takes a sledgehammer and starts to hit it. Hull watches, then joins in, and the sound of the two swinging their hammers draws the attention of other miners who stop and watch. It is not just a day at work; watching it the others feel they are in the presence of some extraordinary presence. The Mine owner Coy LaHood's (Richard Dysart) son Josh (Christopher Penn) arrives with a giant of a man (Richard Kiel) and tells the Pale Rider it would be in his best interest to leave the miners. Again, in a Christ-like way, the clerical-collar-wearing Pale Rider answers no, saying he has work to do. The giant now gets off his horse and in a show of strength grabs a sledgehammer and breaks the boulder in two. Then, raising the hammer over his head, he turns to hit the mysterious stranger, who, in a move that would have made Butch Cassidy proud, swings his own sledgehammer up between the giant's legs causing quite obvious pain. In loving and gentle fashion he then helps the giant back on his horse, saying, "the lord works in mysterious ways." The humbled giant rides off.

Does this movie suggest the Lord was indeed working in mysterious ways when the giant was knocked to the ground by the Pale Rider? Could this be the story of Paul, who was also something of a brute specializing in punishing and persecuting the helpless? Paul changed his ways and came to the side of Christ. This came about when he was knocked to the ground from his horse by a bolt of bright white light. Paul heard a voice ask why he was persecuting him, and when he asked who "him" was, he heard, "I am Jesus of Nazareth, whom you are persecuting." It would seem the spirit of Jesus was there when Paul fell from his horse, if not actually part of that white light that knocked him down to gain his attention.

The giant, too, was a persecutor of the helpless, in his case the homesteading miners. His ways also changed after he, too, was felled by a Christ-like figure. For Paul the tumble was caused by a bright light. For the giant it was a blow between the legs. Paul got back on his horse, but his life was changed. He stopped persecuting the innocent. The giant got back on his horse and, as we see later, quit persecuting the innocent miners and took a position by the side of the Pale Rider. Two brutes who persecuted others, two epiphanies, two changed men who came to work the other side of the street.

The Pale Rider looks identical (same hat and long coat) to the mysterious stranger in Eastwood's earlier *High Plains Drifter* (1973). But this character was not Christ-like at all, and seemed very much an ungodly avenger, having "committ[ed] three murders and one rape in the first 20 minutes," to quote the video jacket. There is no comparable vengeance here, as, he gently rebuffs the romantic advances of Megan and her mother, both of whom have fallen in love with him, and rescues Megan from being raped by Josh LaHood (Christopher Penn).

Standing quietly listening to Coy LaHood tell him "You're a trouble-maker stranger," the scene feels a little like a movie in which the Roman governor of Judea, Pilate, questions Jesus. LaHood also tempts him by offering to build him a church in town, to which the mysterious stranger quietly declines saying, "I could see how a preacher would be tempted." Whoever he is supposed to be, this mysterious stranger appears to be above worldly temptation. He is not interested in the miner's gold—whereas "the Man with No Name" was certainly intent on finding buried Confederate gold in *The Good, the Bad, and the Ugly*. This time the mysterious stranger is another sort of person. He is not interested in LaHood's temptation, nor Megan and Sarah's love offerings, nor the power that would come from being top gun in a small community. No, such worldly motives do not interest the Pale Rider at all. He has come, it seems, for another purpose:

> Behold, I am coming soon! My reward is with me, and I will give to everyone according to what he has done. I am the Alpha and the Omega, the First and the Last, the Beginning and the End. (Revelation 22-12)

The Pale Rider is much more the Alpha and Omega, the First and Last, a Christ-like figure who has come to judge the conduct of humanity on judgment day.

Throughout most of the movie the Pale Rider judges the conduct of mankind—as symbolized by this small mining community. He sits high on his pale horse ("Then I saw a great white throne and him who was seated on it..."), judging the conduct of Megan, Sarah, Hull, Coy and Josh LaHood ("And I saw the...great and small, standing before the throne....and [they] were judged according to what they had done..." [Revelation 20]). Sitting on his pale horse high upon a hill he watches the spewing high pressure water hose howl like a demon washing away the hillside. Of hydraulic mining, Megan says, "It looks like Hell." He just sits and watches, as if taking in all the facts before rendering a judgment. He then rides into town and comes upon LaHood's men beating the leader of the miners, Hull Barrett. High upon his horse, he watches humanity bickering, fighting, and clearly not following the Lord's commandments. He looks down in judgment for a second or two and the bullies look up, aware they are being watched (and judged?). Oblivious, they return to beating Hull. The stranger reaches a judgment, dismounts, and takes one of the ax handles that they had been beating Hull with, and fights off the mining company bullies. Hull is free and invites the Pale Rider home with him. He later comes across Josh LaHood trying to rape young Megan. Again, he is above it all, sitting high on a hill, on his pale horse (the white throne?) watching, and then, judgment: he intervenes to rescue Megan.

Together these scenes constitute what could be called a visual structure of moral judgment. First, the Pale Rider is always on higher ground, above those being judged, as he looks down on the conduct of humanity. Second, he is always in a passive state of contemplation, weighing both sides of the issue thereby allowing a judgment to be reached. Third, in taking one side or the other, he separates right from wrong and indicates that a judgment has been rendered. Fourth, this is not an instantaneous judgment based on emotion, love, hatred, or material interest. It is a dispassionate judgment, the gaze of God on the conduct of mankind: the rape of the land, the brutality of man to man and men to women. In this microcosm of the human condition we see the full range of human conduct, and it is being judged. Once the conclusions have been reached the judgment is executed. Some will be granted the equivalent of eternal life and others the equivalent of being cast into the lake of fire. So far, no one has died at the hands of the Pale Rider. But now the classic western ending of a shootout hints at Christ's return to execute God's judgment.

The magnitude of the judgment is heightened when LaHood hires the ruthless Stockburn (John Russell) and his six deputies. He is a wicked marshall for hire. It is as if LaHood is eliciting the aid of the Devil and his six demons to do battle with the Christ-like Pale Rider.

Stockburn and the Pale Rider have both heard of each other. It is like good and evil being aware of the other's presence. Stockburn says he knows the Pale Rider, but thought he was dead (earlier Eastwood is shown taking off his shirt revealing five or six bullet scars on his back). It seems Stockburn had tried to kill him before and failed. These forces of good and evil were not only aware of each other but had fought before, and their final gunfight seems a battle between good and evil on a cosmic scale. "Its an old score and time to settle it," says the Pale Rider riding off to meet Stockburn. In the final gun battle, the final judgment day comes to pass. On the basis of their conduct, judgment is rendered.

To the destroyer of the earth: death. The Pale Rider throws sticks of dynamite at the water cannons that had assaulted the earth, then at the shushes from which the gold was taken from the earth, and finally at the cabins where the mining company men lived. The mining company, the defiler of God's earth, is destroyed. Eternal life is granted the earth.

To good Hull Barrett: life. He wants to join in the battle against LaHood, but the Pale Rider scares away his horse so he cannot follow and therefore will not risk death in a gunfight.

To LaHood and henchmen: death. In town LaHood's men see the Pale Rider go into a coffeehouse to eat. They follow, guns blazing at the table where he was sitting, but he isn't there. Like a spirit he disappears and then reappears off to their left. Some flee and are granted life. Others reload and draw their guns. The Pale Rider shoots and they are given death. LaHood, himself, is later killed.

To Stockburn the devil and his six demons: death. The Pale Rider stands in the middle of the street right in front of LaHood's office. Stockburn and deputies see him, and come out on the porch, but as a sign of his otherworldliness the Pale Rider is now gone, leaving only his hat on the ground where he once stood. The deputies go to find him. He kills them all. That leaves Stockburn. They face each other in the street. In classic western form, Stockburn draws first but the Pale Rider beats him to the draw, and at that instance Stockburn calls out "You, You." He recognizes the face of the Pale Rider as perhaps the face of God, Christ, or an avenging angel, as he now, at the moment of his death, sees his judge and executioner.

Judgment has been rendered and the Pale Rider leaves town, riding out the same way he rode in. Megan has arrived in town and runs after the Pale Rider: "Preacher....We all love you preacher. I love you. Thank you. Good bye." She then turns and walks back to town, and the Pale Rider disappears over the horizon from whence he came.

A.J.B.

Notes

1. Richard Schickel, *Clint Eastwood: A Biography* (New York: Vintage, 1996), p. 404.
2. Ibid., p. 404.

8

Ghost

Think of the most touching love story you ever saw. Think, too, of the brightest comedy, the most astonishing supernatural tale, and a sleek mystery-thriller. Did you come up with four separate films? Or are you among the millions of fans and critics who have discovered *Ghost*, the number one film of 1990?

Ghost will surprise you, delight you, make you believe. Patrick Swayze plays a ghost who teams with a psychic (Whoopi Goldberg) to uncover the truth behind his murder—and to rescue his sweetheart (Demi Moore) from a similar fate. "The word of mouth is that *Ghost* is a 'must-see' romance," says *Entertainment Weekly*. "Ditto to that!" (quoted from *Ghost* video cover).

It certainly is about love. The passion of love is fixed in our minds forever in the scene in which Patrick Swayze slides behind Demi Moore sitting at her potter's wheel to lovingly enmesh his hands with her slippery, wet, clay-covered fingers as they erotically massage a piece of supple clay. And if that wasn't enough, "Unchained Melody" ("Oh, my love, my darlin', I hungered for your touch...") is being sung plaintively by the Righteous Brothers. That song and that image are forever fused in our collective memory.

This movie is clearly a powerful love story and in that sense Patrick Swayze and Demi Moore in *Ghost* are similar to Humphrey Bogart and Ingrid Bergman in *Casablanca* or Leonardo DiCaprio and Kate Winslet in *Titanic*. Like these movies *Ghost* is also about interrupted love, subsequent heartbreak, and a deep longing to be reunited. Like *Casablanca* the loss of love appears early in the story, although Demi Moore doesn't mysteriously leave Patrick Swayze to be with another man (as Ingrid

Bergman did to Humphrey Bogart). Nor is the heartache the result of a loved one's death at the end of the movie, as when Leonardo DiCaprio dies in icy North Atlantic waters clinging to the raft on which he has placed Kate Winslet as the *Titanic* sank. In *Ghost* Patrick Swayze is killed by a mugger on the streets of New York, at the beginning of the movie, and most of the story is about the anguish of lost love. Like Bogart losing Ingrid Bergman, Demi Moore is now depressed and deeply saddened by Swayze's death. She misses her lost love terribly. But unlike *Casablanca* we have here a story of love lost by both the survivor and the victim of a murder, who is now a ghost.

As there have been love stories before so have there been ghost stories in the movies. But this ghost is not out to scare and frighten people or haunt houses (although some of that happens to the bad guys at the end). Mostly what Patrick Swayze does as a ghost is express the pain and loss of his greatly loved Molly. If there was a way to count the different expressions on Swayze's face, the vast majority of them would have been sorrow and anguish, reflecting the full range of his love's pain and its desire to somehow make contact with Demi Moore. If there is such a thing as a lovesick ghost, this opens the door to a portrayal of the ways and passions of eternal love (God?). He died, that is his body died, but his love lived; his love for Molly transcended his death and is as strong or stronger in his afterlife.

What this movie is really about is the desire and passion of eternal love. Sam's constant efforts to make contact, to let Molly know that he loves her, that he is there, and that love never dies, is the primary subject of this movie. *Ghost* suggests there is a caring and a concern for us that transcends death and is eternal. Could this eternal love be a metaphor for God? Eternal love and God have always seemed interchangeable, such that a movie about the presence of such love seems to hint at the same time of the presence of God's eternal love. The presence of such eternal love is virtually the central actor in this movie. Working through the anguished faces of Sam and Molly, longing love is on the screen almost constantly. It is what we feel and what touches us. It is what drives Sam in endless efforts to reach out to Molly and somehow let her know that eternal love not only exists and passionately cares for her, but is constantly trying to demonstrate its care and concern. Such eternal love the film suggests cannot be divided and Molly and Sam find their emotions, thoughts, and feelings inextricably drawn to each other. Love does everything it can to stay intact and defy death. This determines the story line.

Spirits from the afterlife can take on almost any number of qualities; They can be evil, scary, vengeful, witty, funny, happy. In *Ghost* the most dramatic quality of this ghost is a deep longing love for another, which is constantly trying to make contact with that loved one. This, then, is not Richard Dreyfuss in *Always,* who takes his flippant carefree attitude into the afterlife and has to be instructed, by Audrey Hepburn (the metaphoric representation of God) that being a spirit or ghost entails responsibilities. She tells him he must be an instructor for up-and-coming pilots and let go of his attachment to Holly Hunter—his equivalent love interest. She needs to be freed of her attachment to him so she can go on and love again with, as it turns out, the very pilot that Richard Dreyfuss must take under his ghostly wing. He himself needs to be freed of her to rest fully in peace. Swayze also appears as a spirit and like Dreyfuss is still in love with his girl. He, though, is not told to help other colleagues, as was Dreyfuss. In fact, he doesn't do much of anything except cling to Demi Moore. Dreyfuss wondered what to do next in his afterlife, but Swayze had no such freedom, for his love is so all encompassing that he has no choice but to stay by her side.

Grace Experiences

If the world is awash with hints of our being ultimately loved and cared for, then this movie is about just such a world of grace experiences. Patrick Swayze in ghost form is the embodiment of such eternal love, and his efforts to touch Demi Moore are nothing but grace experiences—worldly hints of a love that never dies. For example, Sam discovers that Molly's cat can sense his presence as a ghost and he startles the cat, making it jump to scare off a killer who threatens Molly. He also discovers a psychic, Oda Mae (Whoopi Goldberg), who can hear him and gets her to try and convince Molly of his enduring love. When Oda Mae, the angelic intermediary, isn't successful Sam confronts a ghost he met on the subway who can make objects move, and asks him to teach him so he can push a penny up the inside wall of Molly's apartment to convince her of his loving presence.

Does such eternal love actually scare cats to leave us a sign? Does such love make friends tell us this or that to bring up a memory of being loved? And does such love move objects to give a hint of love's presence? This movie suggests the answer is yes. In a way, Swayze's ghost represents the determined will of eternal love. Such love the movie assures us never rests until it finds a way to reach out to let us know of its loving presence. We have often spoken of such grace experiences in this book, but this is the first time I have seen a formal attempt at depicting eternal love itself trying to break through to tell of its passionate concern.

From this perspective, Swayze's unending efforts to connect with Demi Moore symbolize the unending efforts of eternal love to love us, and a belief in such a sacramental world is a belief in the presence of hints of God's eternal love. Swayze the ghost is by definition eternal. As a ghost passionately in love, he is, by definition, a manifestation of eternal passionate love and is constantly trying to reach out and leave signs of his love. Therefore, what this movie suggests is passionate eternal love (God?), is, by its very nature, constantly trying to give us signs and hints of its loving concern. For Molly the hints of Sam's eternal love were the startled cat—she called out "Sam?" almost sensing his presence—a penny that moved, and some remembrances of Sam relayed by a stranger, Oda Mae.

The Story Line

There is a story too, that fleshes out and grounds the general points made above. The movie opens with Sam and Molly refurbishing a New York loft to build an apartment. Holding hands, kissing, nuzzling, they are clearly very much in love. As they walk home one night, Molly expresses her love for Sam and he says, "Ditto." She's frustrated that he never says "I love you" the way she does. He tells her people who say that don't really mean it. There is a moral arc here that Sam will pass through, for by movie's end he will realize and express his love. They next encounter a mugger (Willy Lopez) who pulls a gun and Sam is fatally shot. But we don't immediately realize this. We see Willy running away with Sam chasing him down a wet street. Willy gets away. Sam stops, turns, and heads back to Molly, only to see her bloodied hands cradling his wounded body in her lap. Sam now realizes he has become a spirit or ghost and can't believe his eyes. In a state of disbelief, shock, and horror, he watches Molly hold his body. This disbelief is a wonderful device for dramatizing his presence on a spiritual plane. He thinks he is part of the world, when he isn't, yet he doesn't fully accept his identity as a spirit. Molly calls out, "Somebody help us" and he has a pained look on his face; he wants to help but he can't, there is nothing he can do. He reaches out to touch Molly but his hand goes right through her. Staring down at his body, he is shocked that he is now part of some spirit world.

At this point we know Sam's spirit will not leave her side; this is a love that will not be broken, yet its eternal nature is not as yet fully realized by either Sam or Molly. Their love is so strong he cannot let go, which is dramatized when a tunnel of light with what looks like snowflakes floating down, descends from the sky to encircle Sam. It appears to be his time to move on to Heaven. He looks up, as if he is ready to go. Then Molly, still trying to revive his body, cries out, "Sam! Don't you leave me, Sam!" He turns from the light and looks longingly at her and in that moment makes the decision not to leave. The heavenly light now evaporates, leaving the ghost standing alone on a wet New York street.

There is something of a mixed message here. Sam's love is so strong that he cannot leave Molly, yet he is dead, and like Richard Dreyfuss in *Always,* he must let go of her for both their sakes. In death is rebirth, and by not letting go both Sam's and Molly's rebirth is delayed. Sam does not yet fully realize that love is within, and won't disappear with death. For him now, love is attachment, and he refuses to let go, a lot like Richard Dreyfuss refused to let go of Holly Hunter in *Always.*

After attending Sam's funeral Molly is back in her loft, working at her pottery wheel, talking to herself about how much she misses Sam: "Picked up your shirts...think about you every minute. It's as if I can still feel you." At first we don't know what has happened to Sam but then we see him sitting over there on a window sill, looking mournful. He doesn't know what to do. He can't let go, so he lingers; not a stalker or a vagrant, but simply a soul hanging on, incapable of accepting that death and rebirth are one and the same with love transcending both.

Sam later comes across a slightly shady but full of life and loveable psychic, Oda Mae (Whoopi Goldberg) who it turns out can hear his voice. He hounds her until she agrees to serve as an intermediary with Molly. As Andy Greeley reminded me, Whoopi Goldberg is like a seraphim, an angel, a bridge, connecting the eternal love that is Sam to the living that is Molly. While humans may believe the world is full of hints of eternal love, it doesn't mean they will always see them, and in this case Molly does not believe any of this. It all seems too far-fetched.

Having learned how to make objects move Sam tries again to make contact with Molly, this time moving a penny with his finger up the inside wall of her apartment.

Through most of the movie we have seen things through Sam the ghost's eyes. We have felt his anguish at losing Molly, his disbelief that he is a spirit/ghost, and his multiple efforts to reach out and touch her. It has been from the point of view of eternal love (Sam) trying to reach through the divide of death and leave messages on the other side.

Now the point of view shifts to the object of love's attention: Molly. We now see things through her eyes. We see how a grace experience might look to someone who was experiencing it. There are no visible spirits, ghosts, or angels on the screen—we can't see Sam. It is now from Molly's point of view. She sees a penny move mysteriously up the wall then float, in mid-air, across the room toward her. Like a miracle, or a very profound grace experience, Molly now believes a message has been left by someone on the other side. She now believes in the presence of Sam's eternal love. Tears well up in her eyes and the divide that was death is bridged, as the love on one side is about to be reunited with the love on the other. We now see Sam. He sits beside Molly on the couch. She, of course, can't see him, and just looks forward: "Sam, can you feel me?" Oda Mae, translating for Sam: "He says with all his heart....Wishes he were alive so he could touch you." Oda Mae then tells him to enter her body and use it as a medium to physically touch Molly. From Oda Mae's hand touching Molly's we go to Sam and Molly caressing each other. It is a cinematic statement of the power of love to defy death and realize its eternal nature.

At this point Carl, Sam's co-worker and supposed friend who hired Willy to kill him, breaks into the loft apartment, and chases Molly and Oda Mae. Sam jumps out of Oda Mae's body as soon as Carl banged on the door. Now, with his ability to move objects, Sam is able to strike Carl and they fight. Carl crashes into a window and is killed by a huge piece of falling glass. Carl's spirit now leaves his body, and it is soon surrounded by groaning black shrouded spirits from Hell, who whisk him off to the underworld.

Molly and Oda Mae are now safe, and Sam calls out, "Are you two allright?" "Sam?" says Molly, "I can hear you." They have connected across the divide of death. The heavenly light from above once again comes down and surrounds Sam. He glows radiantly in white light. Molly sees the light too and with its golden colors flickering on her face she says in pure awe, "Oh, God," as she now seems to be able to see Sam. She leans forward for a kiss, and his glowing presence leans down as spirit and flesh touch, as if to kiss. They are connected for a moment. Being the angel she is—who in fact does know what is coming next, Oda Mae now says, "They're waiting for you Sam." This time he does not stay. Both are now freed from their possessive attachment to each other. There is now a deeper sense of certainty that they are together, even though apart. Turning to Molly, Sam says, "I love you Molly, I've always loved you"—the very phrase he said he would never utter. "Ditto" she replies, using his old phrase. He says he loves her and he lets go of her at the same time, and it seems to be due to something more than just Molly's safety, which he has insured by disposing of Willy and Carl. Love as protection and care are important, of course, but it seems that they have both come to a more deeper spiritual understanding of love. He realizes its eternal nature. Death is not the end and he can go on. She learns to believe in grace experiences, hints of love's larger continuity. Both are now set free in the eternity of their love.

He begins to back into the light behind him, and stops: "It's amazing, Molly, love is inside you, you take it with you." With tears of joy and love flowing from her reddened eyes, she watches him turn and walk into the white light, where he appears to be welcomed by barely visible white figures. It is an ending taken from *Close Encounters of the Third Kind* where all the white creatures surrounded Richard Dreyfuss walking onto the alien spaceship. Here the metaphor is used for those already in Heaven whom Sam is joining.

A.J.B.

9

Flatliners: Forgiveness Stronger than Death

Flatliners is a film about life after death. A band of five young medical students determine to solve the last and final mystery—death. They
induce death in one another so that they might undergo Near Death
Experiences and report back on their systematic experiments to the rest
of the world. Their arrogant youthful inexperience, particularly as dis-
played by Nelson (Kiefer Sutherland) represents the arrogance of science, a frequent target in contemporary films. However, the film goes
far beyond that cliché to ask what might happen in the NDE world. It
also introduces a malign dimension of NDE which does not appear in
the literature on the subject.

The NDE was barely known at the time of *All That Jazz* in 1979.
Eleven years later at the time of *Flatliners* it was common knowledge.
A few years later in the 1990s the tunnel leading to a figure in light had
become almost a cliché. The four young people—Nelson, Rachel (Julia
Roberts), David Lambraccio (Kevin Bacon), and Joe Hurley (William
Baldwin) never make it to the tunnel. Indeed they are short-circuited at
the "life-review" stage where crimes of the past come back to haunt
them, first in the NDE state and then in ordinary consciousness after
they have aborted the NDE. They are stopped at the phase in which Joe
Gideon encounters Angelique—judgment. The verdicts against them
are harsh. The Reality behind judgment does not seem nearly so affectionate or tolerant as Angelique.

The plot is complicated by a love triangle involving the three troubled
principals—Nelson, Rachel, and David. Nelson is arrogant, contemptuous, ambitious, insufferable. Rachel is haunted by death and eagerly
interviews hospital patients who have had brushes with death to learn

what the experiences were like. David is a bitter, hard-nosed skeptic who has been fired from the hospital because he operated on a woman though he was not qualified to do so. He saved her life but that made no difference, especially since he upstaged a doctor whose late arrival would have been too late to save the woman. He can reapply and will, his friends tell him, be readmitted because he is so good at what he does. But disillusioned and sickened by the system, he insists that he is through with medicine.

The film begins with Loyola University campus looming up as the camera rushes across Lake Michigan. The rest of the story of *Flatliners* is also filmed in Chicago, but a Chicago that is barely recognizable even on the third or fourth viewing. The city dissolves into dark corners, wet alleys, shabby apartments, dingy elevated trains, and dreary university buildings, complete with ominous gargoyles. The hospital where the young doctors work is nothing like the modern hospitals one sees in *Chicago Hope* or *ER*. Rather it is a grim, old-fashioned place, Edwardian or even Victorian, the kind of hospital one might see in a film about veterans of the Great War recovering in London.

Small wonder it's a strange sort of hospital. It is a temporarily converted Field Museum of Natural History, normally famous for its massive dinosaur skeletons. Indeed, once I knew the hospital was in fact the museum (or part of it) I tried to find the dinosaurs lurking in the background. The atmosphere of *Flatliners* is so uncanny that almost anything might happen in it.

Chicago is a city which, even at the winter solstice, has more than nine hours of daylight, a fact you would never suspect from watching *Flatliners*. It is a grim, dark, threatening city which makes Belfast look like Paris.

And through it all runs the unrelenting symbol of an elevated train whose roar may well stand for the drab monotony of life, especially when it (presumably the Blue Line, once called the Howard Street line) plunges into the underground darkness of the subway.

The setting of *Flatliners* is essential to the film, much more so than in most films. Director Joel Schumacher tells much of his story by manipulating light and color. Like Bob Fosse in *All That Jazz,* he wants to tell a religious story (perhaps not consciously) about the meaning of life and death and has no repertory of traditional religious symbols on which to rely. This is perhaps just as well because traditional symbols may have muted the power of his work. So he tells much of his story with light (more often darkness) and color. He turns Chicago into an antechamber of hell where men and women skirt closely to the edge of damnation. Perhaps more appropriately Chicago has become Purgatory where the leading characters work out their salvation by seeking forgiveness—though of course the film does not refer to Purgatory.

The photography and interior sets are equally threatening. The life after death scenes are sometimes filmed in grainy black and white with occasional jabs of color. In the operating room where near death experiences are induced, lighting streams through grates on the floors and statues of angels decorate the walls. Heaven and Hell are in mortal combat.

The notion of a time between life and death in which people work out the final details of their salvation runs through many of the "God in the Movies" films. Just as Catholicism, which "invented"[1] Purgatory has abandoned its old emphasis, filmmakers seem to have discovered it.[2] The Chicago of *Flatliners* is the antechamber of hell, but it is also, potentially, the antechamber of heaven.

Much of this symbolism escaped the film critics, as do all religious or quasi-religious symbols in films. The critics are, with some happy exceptions, as religiously illiterate as filmmakers—and even more religiously insensitive. Hence they were generally furious at the "happy ending" tacked on at the end of the film (as they saw it). If there's one thing critics hate, it's a happy ending. But if Joel Schumacher, the director of *Flatliners,* was to be true to the integrity of the NDE, he had to end the film with a powerful note of hope. Moreover, if one is to make a film about forgiveness, it would be anticlimactic to conclude that for some humans, forgiveness is impossible. Schumacher's vision seems to demand that even an obnoxious, cruel so-and-so like Nelson be capable of salvation. In this respect Schumacher's rough and ready theology is compatible with the Christian tradition, even with Thomas Aquinas, to say nothing of Origin, Karl Rahner, and Hans Urs von Balthassar.

No one seems to have noticed that Gotham City in Schumacher's *Batman and Robin* resembles the Chicago of *Flatliners.* While Gotham City was a grim place in previous films in the series, its harshness becomes electric in Schumacher's vision, a cascade of wild and terrifying colors which brought me back to the operating room in the Field Museum, a much more interesting place than the Bat Castle.

Nelson is the first of the medical students to be the subject of the NDE experiment. His temperature is lowered to the freezing level and his brain wave lines on the monitor go flat. After a minute he is revived. His colleagues eagerly demand an explanation. We know from the madly surrealistic images of his flat line experience that he is somehow involved with the death of a young boy and that the boy has haunted him in his interlude of Near Death. He parries his friends, questions with vague descriptions of ecstasy. Then they creep out of the operating room and back to real life, as real as can be in Schumacher's terrifying Chicago. Nelson wanders down dark streets and rainy alleys and encounters his long-dead dog Champ. He is clearly terrified, but we do not know yet of what. But we do begin to realize that the young people are not only playing with death but encountering demonic and dangerous energies.

At this point *Flatliners* becomes a truly scary film. Indeed I found it more terrifying than any of the standard monster or ghost horror films. My nephew Sean had warned me not to miss it. However, in the summer my good intentions are weaker than at other times in the year (not that they are ever all that strong). Finally, after the film's run had ended at all the theaters in the Dune Country, I had no choice but to work up enough energy to drive over to LaPorte Indiana to a theater on the far side of LaPorte to which I had never ventured before. It wasn't easy to find. Driving home after the film, it was even less easy to find my way to Indiana 39. In the city of LaPorte, however, there was enough light so that I did not have to worry about demons lurking in the darkness. Outside of LaPorte, on the road to New Buffalo, the scary shapes were everywhere, sometimes even threatening to run across the road into the glare of my headlights.

None of them did, however. At least I don't think they did. Nonetheless, I was extremely happy when I turned off Highway 12 at the lone streetlight which welcomes me into the familiar haven of Grand Beach. To tell the truth, even Grand Beach seemed haunted that late August night.

Perhaps I went into this spooked slightly "altered" state because I am inclined to occasional interludes of Irish romanticism which knows that the boundaries between this world and the Many Colored Lands are thin and permeable. A more likely explanation (maybe) is that the issue of forgiveness (which, by the way, is the same thing as salvation) with which the film wrestles is one with which one of my vocations inclines me to be preoccupied.

Nevertheless, if one watches *Flatliners* and is not scared, then one is incorrigibly prosaic—and hence might make a good film critic.

Joe Hurley wins the bidding to be the next experimental subject with an offer of one minute and thirty seconds. In wild surrealistic images (which mark all the experiences) he encounters the women he has seduced and whose seductions he has secretly recorded on video tape. Again he is vague about what has happened. Soon, however, he begins to imagine the video tapes of his victims on ordinary television.

Roger Ebert, in his perceptive (as usual) commentary on *Flatliners* suggests that there were one too many NDEs for the coherence of the film. One suspects that there was an intention originally to find forgiveness for Hurley who loses his fiancée when she finds his video tapes, but the filmmakers had the sense not to prolong the film. Moreover, how would he seek forgiveness from each of the women he seduced? It might have been better to exclude the Hurley character completely—though this might have deprived the film of some of its erotic charge. As it is, however, we are left to wonder why he is excluded from the possibility of forgiveness and to wonder what his path to forgiveness might be.

David (Kevin Bacon) is the next one to experiment with death. He purports not to believe in anything. He rejects the experiments as folly. But he goes along with them because of his love for Rachel. When Rachel bids two minutes of death, he outbids her two minutes and thirty seconds. Better to die himself than to lose Rachel to death.

Nelson plays games with the time, perhaps because he wants to get rid of David (who is dying appropriately on Halloween). The others work frantically to revive and succeed in doing so, as Halloween revelers (of the sort I've never seen in Chicago) parade on the streets. In his terrifying, dream-like interlude, he meets an African American child he once tormented on a playground.

Now the images, as surrealistic as ever, intrude violently into the lives of the medical students. The little boy assaults Nelson on the street and injures him. Later he appears in Nelson's apartment and beats him again. Joe's women appear on every television at which he looks, even in a TV store window. The little black girl hurls insults at David on a L train (just as it plunges into the ground). No one else sees the dog or the little boy or the video tapes or the black girl, sins of the past have come alive in the present to haunt the sinners.

Now it is Rachel's turn. I tell my students that it is utterly unthinkable that Julia Roberts, appealingly fragile in a white bra, would have done anything that merited punishment. Sure enough. Her challenge is not to seek forgiveness but to forgive. While "dead" she witnesses the most horrible of all the surrealistic scenes of the group – her father, apparently a career non-com in the army, has become a drug addict. As a little girl she sees him "shooting up." Distraught by the fact that his child has found him out, her father commits suicide with his service revolver. Her mother blames her for his death. While her lines are "flat," water short-circuits the electrical system (the sort of thing which happens when you use the Field Museum for a hospital!) and Rachel is dead for five minutes. With desperate efforts, the group revives her. They decide that their experiments are too dangerous to continue.

Her father now haunts Rachel, just as the little boy haunts Nelson, his women victims haunt Joe and the black girl, Winnie Hicks, haunts David. By messing around with death and activating the images of their past, the medical students have somehow transferred their guilts into ghosts which hunt them with vengeful fury in the "real" world of every day life.

Rachel's guilt, however unwarranted, becomes the ghost of her father who first appears in a bathroom mirror and then as a cadaver she is dissecting for class. Finally the young people overcome their shame and their fear and share experiences with one another. They realize that they must seek forgiveness. David finds out where his playground victim is living and, along with a still skeptical Nelson drives out to the pastoral suburban green house where she and her husband live and work. I'm sure that this idyllic rural setting actually exists somewhere in the Chicago area, but I must warn those who are not familiar with Chicago that it will be hard to find it and it is anything but typical. The sunlit, bucolic scene is a vigorous contrast to the dark, damp city where our students are being tormented. However, Billy Mahoney, the little boy for whose death Nelson was responsible (and spent time in reform school), still manages to appear in the bright light of suburban day and continues to beat up Nelson in the locked pick-up truck while David is in the house.

The woman whom he once mocked in the playground denies all recollection of the event. Happy with her husband and family and free from racism in their pleasant rural environment, she does not want to call up her own painful memories. There is nothing, she insists in a poignant and powerful scene, to forgive. Her husband arrives, a man who looks like a middle-linebacker, and is distinctly unhappy with the white man who seems to be hassling his wife. Finally, and bravely, she smiles and nods her head in forgiveness. David returns to the truck just in time to save Nelson from more punishment at the hands of Billy Mahoney—who, of course, disappears when David arrives.

Meanwhile Rachel encounters her father again, relives his suicide and realizes that it was not her fault. He asks her for her forgiveness which she grants and then he disappears, freed at last from his guilt.

David and Rachel have made their peace with the ghosts their hubris has created. The film forgets about the unfortunate Joe. But what about Nelson? How can he win forgiveness from Billy Mahoney, now that he understands the rules of the game? There is only one way: he must cross the boundaries that separate the living and the dead and seek out Billy. He returns to the hospital (whose security guards must be unconscionably inefficient) and induces death in himself. He again relives the death of Billy, who apparently was strangled by tree branches while running from Nelson. However, Bill is not angry at him. Rather, bathed in a warm light, he smiles happily and goes off with Champ, Nelson's long-lost dog. Released from his long-time torment, Nelson runs back to his life and is revived (after being dead nine minutes) by his anxious friends.

During this last attempt to solve the mystery of death, when it looks like they have lost Nelson, David, the atheist, turns to the window and addresses God. We're sorry we trespassed on your territory, this Italian (and presumably Catholic) non-believer tells the deity, but please let us have him back. God apparently complies.

Were the apparitions of Billy Mahoney, Winnie Hicks, the women on Joe's video tapes, and Rachel's father "real?" Billy and apparently Winnie had already forgiven their tormentors. Rachel's father wanted to be forgiven, but was he really trapped in a Purgatory-like situation? Or did Rachel have to make peace with herself by forgiving the image of her father which was locked in her memory? Did all three of the young need to forgive themselves?

And what about the enigmatic Joe Hurley? Would it be possible that, if he forgave himself for his sleaze, he might persuade the woman he really loved to forgive him?

Do we have to seek forgiveness not only from others but also from ourselves to find a modicum of peace? It is surely true that forgiveness is never complete until we forgive ourselves. If God has forgiven us and the one we have offended has forgiven us, what right do we have to stand in sterner judgment of ourselves than others have? Are the young people in *Flatliners* finally in the same situation as Joe Gideon in *All*

That Jazz? Are they harsher on themselves than others might be? Is their interlude of judgment between life and death, however terrifying it might have been, substantively no different from that of Joe Gideon? Is the Reality which converts their arrogance into humility similar to Angelique?

It is unlikely that Joel Schumacher and Peter Filardi, his screenwriter, considered these questions explicitly. It does not follow, however, that there are not answers to these questions "in front of the text." The film has no interest in the metaphysics of how guilt images of the past can do actual physical harm to Nelson. It seems to act on the premise that in Science Fiction some things need not be explained. My hunch is that the film merely insists on the possibility of forgiveness, a possibility which even death cannot eliminate. It leaves to us the less important question of whether the humans we have offended have already forgiven us. Billy clearly has no more anger towards Nelson, but in the place of light where he (and Champ) live, there can be no grudges. Releasing David from his memories does require effort, albeit healing effort from Winnie. On the other hand, it does not seem likely that the f(F)orgiveness which animates the story would really have left Rachel's father in "Purgatory" until her NDE. Tentatively I suggest that the primary targets of forgiveness are the sinners themselves, but that they need reassurance that others have forgiven them before they can forgive themselves.

However, the important theme of *Flatliners* is that there is forgiveness and that death does not preclude it. The living can forgive the dead. The dead can forgive the living. This overwhelming insight is compatible with the traditional Catholic teaching about the "Communion of Saints." The boundaries between the living and the dead are indeed thin and permeable, just as the Celts believed long before they became Christians (and celebrated on Halloween, the day on which agnostic David plunges into his own past and judgment upon it).

God in *Flatliners* is light—warm, bright light which appears but rarely. When it appears, however, it wraps its characters in happiness. God's gift to the five medical students is forgiveness, a forgiveness which transcends death. Does *Flatliners* believe in life after death? It believes in something even more important—forgiveness which death cannot prevent. Patently if forgiveness survives so do we who forgive and are forgiven, but *Flatliners* sees no need to make that point.

The God in *Flatliners* is Forgiveness.

A.M.G.

Notes

1. The notion of a state between death and new life was part of the Catholic tradition from a much earlier era. However, only in the 13th century did the description of Purgatory as a place emerge, most notably in the work of the monk H of Salton in his description of St. Patrick's Purgatory on Station Island in Ireland's Lough Derg, a place more recently visited by Seamus Heaney.
2. Yet another example of Greely's First Law: When others discover something has traditionally been Catholic, Catholics are in the process of abandoning it.

10

Jacob's Ladder: God in the Nightmare

A filmmaker who wants to wrestle with the "non-obvious" has several different genres within which to work. One can choose simply to select an actor who seems in the context to be a useful if inadequate metaphor for God—Audrey Hepburn, Jessica Lange, George Burns, Lionel Barrymore. Or one can hint at the "non-empirical" by the reflection of God in a person who is utterly devoted to the deity—Marie Falconetti in Dreyer's *Passion of Joan of Arc*. Or one can use a symbol which hints at what God is like—the lacy white cloud in *Truly, Madly, Deeply* or light in many films. One can use a parable in Magical Realism to suggest how God responds to the problem of why bad things happen to good people. One can elect to combine several of these different methods. Each of these techniques is a way of coping with the fact that none of us have seen God and, even if we had seen Her, by definition, She is ineffable and cannot be captured in a work of art. Thus, we must necessarily portray God indirectly—as indeed must the metaphysicians. We all are constrained to metaphors and to choose from a variety of metaphorical styles.

Yet another style of trying to portray the non-observable is to retreat into the world of the preconscious and unconscious. I use the word "retreat" advisedly. In a certain sense the God of dream and fantasy is a God that we cannot (at least for this particular film) depict with a human surrogate or a metaphor or a fable.[1] Therefore we probe into the dark, lower basements of our psyche to release the fluid, transient, flickering, capricious images which stir fear and wonder in the organism. One cannot parse easily the meaning of a work of art built around such images. Perhaps one should not try. They are designed to create moods, hints which are not only not rational, but even nonpropositional. Necessarily these images become inkblots into which viewers (if the images are in one of the visual arts) can read almost, but not quite, whatever they want. The artist (filmmaker in this case) can refuse to say what the images mean on the usual grounds that such is not the artist's job but also add the more basic excuse that he has no idea what they mean —a position close to that Bruce Joel Rubin takes on in his film *Jacob's Ladder.* The images are about light and darkness, hope and terror, good and evil, life and death, sin and redemption, the obvious and the non-obvious. They seem to incline to the hope end of the hope/despair continuum. But beyond those obvious facts, viewers are forced to make up their own minds. They are asked to confront their own unconscious terrors and hopes with the unconscious terrors and hopes of the filmmaker and see what kind of transcendence might be disclosing itself in such terrors and hopes. If it is difficult to understand dream and fantasy films about God, they are also wonderful conversation starters. In the film of William Kennedy's *Ironweed*, for example, there's no doubt about the imagery of a happy death in which Kennedy enfolds the Meryl Streep character (she prays in front of the statue of St. Joseph the patron of a happy death). But what should one make of the imagery of death in *Jacob's Ladder*?

In Roger Ebert's words about the latter film which describes the essence of the fantastical approach to the non-obvious, "what *Jacob's Ladder* really wants to do is to evoke the feeling of a psychological state in the audience. We are intended to feel what the hero feels"—the sheer raw terror of human mortality and the smidgen of hope which lurks indestructible in the terror.

There are few things in *Jacob's Ladder* which are clear. It is a story about a Vietnam veteran, (perhaps) returned from the war but still haunted by demons, sometimes quite literally. Jacob Singer (Tim Robbins), a professor with a Ph.D. (subject unspecified) comes home (maybe) with his ambition shattered. He leaves his wife and children, goes to work at the Post Office, and moves in with one of his co-workers, a woman significantly (perhaps) called Jezie, short for Jezebel (Elizabeth Peòa). Blood-soaked nightmares about a fire fight during the war plague him. He is tormented by the death of a son in an auto accident when, for a moment, he let the son out of his sight. We are not sure whether this was before or after his time "in country." Jezebel destroys his family pictures, because (perhaps) she sees them as a link with his other life.

Jacob is unable to give up his dreams. There have also been, perhaps, a couple of attempts on his life. He must find an explanation. He hunts for his V.A. therapist and discovers that the man has disappeared, indeed according to the records has never existed. Then he learns that the doctor's car blew up. He wonders if he and the men in his outfit were victims of a government experiment with drugs. An army buddy begs to see him. They meet in a pool hall. The buddy has the same kind of dreams. He tells Jacob that he's going to hell. Then the buddy's car blows up. At the man's funeral, he contacts some of his friends who survived the fire fight, all of them haunted by similar dreams. They resolve to discover what happened. But mysterious pressures are brought to bear on them and they back out.

There is a possibility, never clear for most of the film, that much of Jacob's present life is a dream he is experiencing in Vietnam. It is not clear to us because it was not clear to writer Bruce Joel Rubin and director Adrian Lyne, as Rubin discloses in a book about the film. Only when the final cut was made were the two of them satisfied that the film hung together, but even at the end of his book, Rubin seems unsure. *Jacob's Ladder* is a story with two souls.

One is forced to conclude that there were many, perhaps too many, cuts in the editing, so that not only is the story mysterious but at times it is impenetrable. Jezebel's name suggests she is in league with the demons, yet her tenderness with Jacob suggests the opposite. Is she a good force in his life or a bad one? We receive hints in both directions and must make our judgments. I suspect that originally she was cast as a demon and Rubin and Lyne softened her edges and obscured the evidence.

Even before I read Rubin's book, I suspected that those responsible liked the power and the mystery of the story and were reluctant in their own minds to decide how it finally ended, though Roger Ebert, at his masterly best, observed that the ending is less important than the terrors Jacob experiences: "This is a film about no less than life and death, and Jacob seems to stand at the midpoint of a ladder that reaches in two directions. Up to heaven, like the ladder that God put down for the Biblical Jacob in Genesis. Or down the ladder into the hell of drug induced dreams."

Jacob's dreams are indeed surrealistic hallucinations, though perhaps no more surreal than the dreams many of us have. Often in our dreams we are pursued by terror and then, perhaps, turn around and pursue it, trying to route it by brute force. How is Jacob, caught between the living and the dead—it matters not whether in the bright sunny jungles of Vietnam or in grim and shabby New York—to escape the terrors.

The film is set in a perpetually gray, run-down, dirty New York in which it is difficult to know as one watches the film for the first time what is real and what is not. Thus when Jacob is seized with a high fever after a wild party, he imagines that he is back home in bed with his wife (Patricia Kalember) and that he must get up to tuck in his children. Again when he is in the hospital, he is wheeled off to a dark, bloodstained madhouse for x-rays. The doctors seem to be demons determined to torment him. They tell him he is dead and bind him so he cannot move. Jezie is one of them.

Just like Jacob in the Scripture (Genesis: 32), he must wrestle with an angel. In the biblical story, it is night. Jacob is alone on one side of a reader, having his wives and his concubines and his children and his servants and his flock across the river. (Why is he by himself? Don't ask! This is the Bible!). An angel shows up and wrestles with him all night. Neither of them wins. The angel smites him on the hip. Jacob demands to know who the angel is. The angel won't tell him but broadly hints that he is God. Jacob builds a shrine on the spot because, as he says, here he met the living God. One can debate at great length about the meaning of the story, as about the meaning of many of the other stories of the patriarchs. Most modern translations say that Jacob wrestled with a man. The point may be well taken, but it is irrelevant. Jacob thought he had wrestled with God and maybe he had—he had struggled with many humans during his checkered career, why not God? In the Jewish scriptures the Malek Jahweh, the Angel of the Lord, is God appearing in human form.

For the purposes of the story, however, Jacob Singer does wrestle with an angel in the person of his friendly—and well-read—chiropractor Louis (Danny Aiello). The chiropractor is the key person, the revelatory person, in the story. He informs Jacob that Sara (his wife) still loves him. He repeatedly tells Jacob that he must let go of his life if he wants to live again, a theme not unlike that of the Jessica Lange and Audrey Hepburn personages in their films. He might mean that Jacob should stop clinging to life as he dies of his wounds in Vietnam or that he should give up his anger and return to his family and his work. He

and Jacob wrestle, Louis smites him on the hip as part of his chiropractic treatment, and the pain in Jacob's back is eased temporarily. Louis
also asks whether Jacob has seen his wife and children and reminds
him that his wife still loves him. He also quotes Meister Eckhardt on
losing life in order to find it.

During the conversation between Louis and Jacob a halo appears
around Louis's head, a trick of the light in his office perhaps. Or were
Rubin and Lyne playing a game with us, perhaps assuring us that they
knew about Genesis : 32 and that they thought Louis was indeed an angel?
(I missed the halo until several of my students called my attention to it.) To
make sure that we get the point, they have Jacob tell Louis that he looks like
an angel and that he is a "wonder." Modestly, Louis says he knows that.

Danny Aiello as God? Certainly the angel of the Lord, certainly a
reflection of God, certainly God's messenger, certainly God's agent
later in the film when he frees Jacob from demons (or merely insensitive doctors and nurses) in a hospital.

After a lawyer tells Jacob that the government has no record of his
ever being in Vietnam, Jacob is picked up by two government thugs
who push him around and warn him to forget about his army service.
Jacob battles them and escapes from their car. He is injured in his
fall from the car. His wallet is stolen by a Santa Claus who took it
out of his pocket while Jacob lay on the street. He is carted off to a
hospital (almost as ugly as the one in *Flatliners* and all the more
depressing because it is real) as an unknown person. Perhaps the
hospital is part of the plot, perhaps the doctors and nurses are on the
side of the demons, but one can't be sure what is dream and what is
real. Sara (the biblical Jacob's grandmother was Sara, not his wife)
and sons comes to visit him. They still love one another. Then Louis,
doubtless informed by Sara, in full soteriological fury storms into
the hospital, frees Jacob from the contraptions that imprison him on
the bed, takes Jacob back to his office and heals his injured back.
Jacob returns to Jezie, not Sara, and reviews his papers. He indeed
was in Vietnam. Finally, a chemist contacts him secretly and tells
him that he developed the drug that was supposed to make American soldiers super-killers, a drug appropriately called The Ladder
because it plunged you straight down into hell. The experiment failed
when the soldiers turned on one another.

The film concludes enigmatically. After hearing from the chemist
what really happened in Vietnam—that the drugged Americans killed

one another—Jacob takes a cab "home" to Brooklyn, to the apartment building where his wife lives. The doorman greets him and welcomes him back. The parlor has the look of a place that is lived in—schoolbooks and partially eaten food. Jacob seems to drift off into a reverie. When the sun rises and bathes the room in light he sees his son sitting at the bottom of the staircase playing with a toy. They go upstairs together where, perhaps, his wife is waiting. The son however, is the one who died. The medics in Vietnam cover his face. He fought bravely against death, they say, but finally he had to let go of life.

Either way Jacob has learned Louis's lesson. He lets go of life in order to find it. He either dies in the military hospital in Vietnam or he dies to his fears and his haunted dreams and his fight with the government to return to his family.

There are problems with either ending. It is hard to believe that Louis, Jezebel, Jacob's wife, the post-office job, the government plot (about which he couldn't have known in Vietnam)—all of which are part of his postwar life—were creations of his dying dreams in the field hospital. Indeed such a conclusion to the story means that most of the rest of it never happened. Despite Roger Ebert, I find this ending offensive every time I see it. It is, I tell myself, a copout, a trick. They have not played fair with us.

One can choose either ending because Lyne and Rubin were not able to make up their minds which ending was most appropriate, though towards the end they inclined to the one which had him die in Vietnam. My students overwhelmingly opt for that outcome, untroubled by the fact that even the most realistic scenes in the film are then written off as dreams and that Louis doesn't exist. I tell them they're wrong. I'm the full professor and that's that. Don't we get a vote, they demand. Not at the University of Chicago, I tell them. Besides, even Ph.D. that he is, how likely is Jacob to hear the quotation from Meister Eckhardt unless he really meets Louis?

It is a foolish argument, though lots of fun. It is also, pace Ebert, beside the point. With the help of Louis (and Meister Eckhardt!) Jacob Singer is able to exorcise the terrors that have been bedeviling (in the strict sense of the word) him. Perhaps the central insight of *Jacob's Ladder* is that the demons, the nightmares, the horrors which plague us are not strong enough to destroy us. No power in heaven or on the earth or under the earth will separate us from the Living God. The God of *Jacob's Ladder* is the God who delivers us from evil.

Mr. Destiny: A Daydream Comes True

Do not pray for something you want badly, goes the ironic dictum, you may get it. In slightly different language, should your daydreams become real, they might turn into nightmares.

That's the lesson Larry Burrows learns in the 1991 film, *Mr. Destiny* (written and directed by James Orr). Like all of us he indulges in daydreams. What would his life be like if he had not struck out in the final inning of a high school baseball championship and cost his team the title? How much different and how much better would his life have been if he had hit a home run!

What would life have been like if I had gone to law school? If I had married that attractive person who seemed interested in me? If I had moved to another city? If I had asked that young man (woman) to the prom? If my parents had not discouraged me from attending college? If I had studied harder for Mstat exams? If I had quit my terrible job?

Indeed, your life might be a lot better. Or it might be a lot worse. Regrets over missed opportunities, like tears over spilt milk, are not only bootless, they are also ungrateful because they ignore the opportunities which you might have closed off if you went (or were permitted to go) in the opposite direction.

In the case of Larry Burrows he was not given much of a choice. Just as he was about to swing the bat for the hit which would have won him fame and glory, a light flashes in his eye, temporarily blinding him. After that he seems doomed to mediocrity. He loses the attention of Cindy Jo, the daughter of the richest man in town (Rene Russo, who also commands the attention of my male students). He ends up with a mediocre middle-level job in her father's company while she marries an athlete who is Larry's boss—a nice man, but not too bright, not nearly as smart as Larry who sniffs out a plot to steal and sell the company but can do nothing about it.

Mind you, he does marry the young woman who consoles him after his strike-out. However, Ellen is now a union activist who seems to have little interest any more in her dull, defeated husband. Moreover, it's his birthday and everyone has forgotten. The high-level executive who is plotting to take over the company fires Larry. Despondent, Larry goes for a ride in his battered old car—all he can afford—which breaks down in a strange part of town which he has never visited before. Looking for help, he stumbles into a strange tavern—called the Universal Joint—and encounters a bartender named Mike (Michael Caine). Larry pours out his soul to Mike: if only he had hit the home run everything would be different. His present life is so ordinary, so dull, so uninteresting. Mike, resplendent in a bow tie, vest and sleeve garters, says that it might just be possible to arrange that, mixes up a smoky drink for Larry, called Spilt Milk and pours it into a large glass, where it continues to smoke. Figuring that he has nothing to lose, Larry swallows the drink and everything changes. He now lives in the alternative reality, one in which he has hit the home run.

It's a Wonderful Life? Patently! And not nearly as good a film, though Michael Caine in the angel role (not for nothing is he called "Mike") instead of Henry Travers is a startling idea. Mike in fact claims to be little bit more. Doubling in brass as "Mr. Burrows" chauffeur, Mike delivers him to his "home," a millionaire's palace. Who are you, Larry demands, an angel or something?

Not exactly, Mike replies. Let's say that I'm the one who lays out the alternatives from which you choose. As he says this, Mike points a finger in the air and makes a small circle of tiny stars. God, in other words, writes the scenarios and we, helped by God's hints, elect which one to follow.

Sometimes.

It's all real, Mike insists. Trust me!

Mike repeats these words often during Larry's excursion into what might have been, hinting perhaps that he has another agenda.

Do you do this often, Larry asks—rearrange people's lives. I make some adjustments, Mike says modestly.

Larry wasn't given much of a choice when he was sixteen. Now he's given a choice. Almost at once he doesn't like it. He has become a thoroughly unpleasant man, disliked and feared by his employees and unloved by his two children. His sexy wife Cindy Jo, who is not all that swift, adores him—though as Larry discovers he is routinely unfaithful to her. Ellen, married to someone else, hates him because he has made passes at her. His old friends despise him. Larry has everything he ever wanted but he has lost everything that mattered to him. His daydream has come true and turns out to be a nightmare.

After several comic mishaps which turn out to be tragic, Larry is accused of murdering his father-in-law. Fleeing from the police he stumbles back into the Universal Joint. Mike is nowhere to be seen.

Larry mixes his own drink. The other reality returns. Mike appears. Larry tells him that his point has been made.

The experience has changed Larry. No longer is he afraid. He has given up sorrow over what might have been and now enjoys what is. He dashes off to the company's board meeting, takes on the senior executive who is trying to destroy the company and routes him. He doesn't wait for the results. He returns to his home in search of Ellen whom he now loves more than ever. The house is dark and quiet. Ellen has gone to bed. She didn't even remember that it was his birthday.

Everyone in the audience knows what's going to happen. He opens the door, the lights go on, SURPRISE! He realizes how good his life has been and how much he means to so many people. Then Cindy Jo and her real husband arrive to wish him happy birthday and to tell him that he has indeed prevented the coup against the firm and to offer him the job of executive vice president. And a new Mercedes. An extra bit of frosting on the cake.

Sentimental? Artificial? Indeed. However, so is *It's a Wonderful Life*. After the guilt and the horrors of *Flatliners* and *Jacob's Ladder*, *Mr. Destiny* seems like kitsch, though Michael Caine is wonderful in the role of the deity, a God of enormous self-confidence and power. Moreover, Larry Burrows had to face his own kind of horror: in his alternate life he is no longer the man he thought he was, not better indeed, but much worse. We know that, like Jimmy Stewart, he will return to his old life, wiser and happier. But he doesn't know that.

The last scene of the film returns to the ball park in a stereotypical stadium-after-the-game setting. The young Larry is sitting in the stands, staring glumly at the empty playing field. Mike appears behind him.

Don't worry, kid, it will all work out. Trust me!

Larry stumbles to his feet and trudges down the stairs. A lot that old fart knows, he mutters.

The audience laughs. By now they understand who the old fart is. He does indeed know a lot. Perhaps about our lives too. The God of *Mr. Destiny* is, like Michael Caine, a God who knows what he's doing, a God who can insist that we should trust him. It is a light touch response to nightmare and horror, but it is the same touch which glows through the dark mirror of the guilt of *Flatliners* and the paralyzing terror of *Jacob's Ladder*. Not only does the God of movies love us, not only does he pursue us relentlessly. She also, if we believe these films of fantasy and nightmare, knows what She's doing. The God of dreams is not all that different from the God of Magical Realism.

Again we must note with some astonishment that all three filmmakers–Schumacher, Lyne, Orr—are wrestling with ultimate questions. The films are all theological. They are intended to be entertaining and to make money, but the first two are also grimly serious and the third makes a point which, however obvious, humankind cannot hear too often. In a world in which so many theologians are interested only in politics and so many clergy are interested only in their own rules and regulations, it is the filmmakers who, like Jacob Singer, wrestle with God.

A.M.G.

Note

1. In the third film in this chapter, a human character does play God. However, it is a film about a very different kind of dream world than that we encounter in the first two.

11

Angel Angst and the Direction of Desire

Angels have a long history in the movies,[1] and how we picture them varies with time and place. As centuries ago, they are still God's messengers, aiding, guiding, and helping humanity. We seem to see them less with wings, and almost never with halos (Danny Aiello's light above his head as he wrestles with Jacob in *Jacob's Ladder* is more an exception). Angels today are imagined more as ordinary people. There are helpful and avenging angels, and they take a wide range of forms. Clint Eastwood's classic character, "the man with no name," plays something of an avenging angel in *High Plains Drifter* returning to the town of Lago to punish townspeople who had allowed the sheriff to be whipped to death by three outlaws. He shoots some, rapes another, and humiliates all, and in the end has them paint their town red, which is then set afire, creating a clear, if quite heavy-handed, metaphoric representation of a town sent to burn in hell. Clint Eastwood returns as the *Pale Rider*, who can certainly be seen as an avenging angel arriving after a young girl prays for assistance to rout demons who are destroying the earth (a vicious mining company) and terrorizing honest miners.

The basic notion of angels, as messengers of heavenly guidance or vengeance, has remained largely intact over the centuries, and in this sense there is nothing new in the religious imagination. But, the distinctly metaphoric nature of religious representations means the imagining process is open to influences of historical context and religious tradition. We have been examining the different ways contemporary society represents religious ideas on the screen, from George Burns in *Oh, God!* to flashes of light in *Fearless*. If, for instance, the middle ages imagines God as being like a great King today he can be imagined as being like a little old man in a windbreaker and yachting cap, which raises the question of what changes that produces in the religious imagination. Obviously social change, different conditions, cultures, and human beliefs about ultimate things all shape our religious imagination, and it can be argued that our religious imagination shapes our views of ourselves and the universe. But for the moment stay a while with the first assumption that the way we view ourselves and the world colors our religious imagination.

What would this mean? At a minimum we could hypothesize that our views of our own nature and psychological essence will be read into our religious imagination. Our sense of the importance of authority being approachable to be effective is perhaps related to the appearance of a representation of God as a kindly little old man like George Burns. The same holds for images of angels too, and in this regard I would like to consider three movies involving angels since the 1930s in terms of how heaven, earth, angels and death all go together as part of a cosmological whole that lies at the heart of any religious imagination.

To explore these interrelationships I will begin with a suggestion by Philippe Aries in his book *The Hour of Our Death* (1981) that Western societies have gone from being much more comfortable and familiar with death in the Middle Ages and early modern times to virtually denying its existence and banishing it from sight today, as we no longer die communally among friends, but alone in a hospital or retirement home.

To create a contrast with the meaning of death today Aries outlines the ideal of a more traditional death in the Middle Ages, what he calls the "tame death." Its essential characteristic was that it gave warning. "'Ah, my good lord, think you then so soon to die? 'Yes,' replies Gawain, 'I tell you that I shall not live two days.' Neither his doctor nor his friends nor the priests...know as much about it as he. Only the dying man can tell how much time he has left" (Aries, 1981: 6). This sort of self-diagnosis, of course, is not infallible. Remember the Indian chief in the Dustin Hoffman film *Little Big Man* who in this grand tradition announced it was his time to die and went up on a hill and lay down to die. But he didn't, and when it started to rain, he had to sit up and go home. Along with announcing one's own death the dying also summoned friends, family and relatives to surround him at his death bed. One did not want to die alone, which, ironically, is probably the most common form of death today. The dying person next makes necessary arrangements, beginning with the ritual recollection of his achievements and regrets. He asks the forgiveness of friends and then takes their leave commending them to God, and after a farewell to the world, commends his own soul to the Lord. In *Gone with the Wind* the death-bed scene of Melanie Hamilton (Olivia DeHavilland) was exactly this. Rhett Butler (Clark Gable), Scarlett O'Hara (Vivien Leigh), Ashley Wilkes (Leslie Howard) and others wait outside her room for their turn to go to Melanie's bedside to hear her final words and pass on their own.

But this does not seem to be the case today. Medicine, in the role of the doctor, now informs of impending death. Still, one could accept and be at peace. But this doesn't seem to be the normative response either. When informed of death there seems to be little resignation or acceptance, only denial and fear, hoping the diagnosis was a mistake and a request for more tests. It's almost as if there are two models of the relationship of heaven to earth that underlie Aries "tame" and what could be called the "denial death" of today. To visualize this, imagine a two-room house where one room hangs over a cliff. The first room represents the world of earthly existence, the second the world of an eternal afterlife, with death being the doorway connecting the two rooms in a larger cosmological framework. In such a construction death is a status passage which seems natural and inevitable, hence the acceptance and resignation of Aries "tame death," for the passage from life to afterlife is still within a larger more encompassing reality.

For a picture of the second heaven/earth model imagine the second room disappearing, representing a waning belief in the real possibility of an afterlife. In this cosmological framework the doorway of death now opens to the emptiness and endless void at the edge of the cliff— the security of belief in the other room of eternal existence is now gone. Where death was previously a transition point within the larger framework of the common cosmological house, it is now an end point, as the here and now of this world (the first room) is no longer an antechamber to eternity (the second room). From the point of view of this cosmological outlook the here and now is all there is or will ever be. Death is now an opening to nothingness, and the anomic terror associated with social margins and ill-defined areas becomes increasingly associated with death. Let's examine some movies in terms of this framework.

Topper (1937)

I begin with the Norman Z. McLeod movie *Topper*, a 1937 comedy starring Cary Grant and Constance Bennett, who play George and Marion Kirby, two carefree and wealthy socialites who die in an auto accident and continue to exist as ghosts waiting to go to heaven. Their attitude toward a heavenly afterlife is established very early on. Their sports car blows out a tire on a turn and they swerve off the road and crash. Both die, and we see their ghost-like spirits leave their bodies and walk over to a log where they sit down and start to talk about the crash not yet fully aware of their spiritual status. But as they start to fade out in each other's eyes, they realize they are now ghosts which raises the question of what to do next in their new condition. They look at each other. George (Cary Grant) suggests they await some trumpets and off they go. But nothing happens. He then goes on to explain to Marion (Constance Bennett) that what you do is tell people your good deeds and they open the heavenly gates. That makes sense, but they cannot think of any good deeds they had done. Maybe it was too late. "Maybe not. Maybe if we could do a good deed now," suggests Marion, and they think of their cautious, conservative, banker Cosmo Topper (Roland Young) and his wife (Billie Burke) who keeps him on a short leash. "His whole soul is crying out for self-expression," Marion says, and so the two of them generate some 1930s madcap movie adventures involving the reluctant, cautious, and stuffy Cosmo that ends up bringing him and his wife closer together—which turns out to be George and Marion's good deed. In the final scene, Topper is recovering in a hospital bed and reconciling with his wife while George and Marion are waiting around up on the roof. They then lean over and look into the window, and, seeing Topper and his wife happy with each other, George catches Topper's eye and says, "So long Toppee, we're on our way."

On their way to heaven, that is. Now remember for a moment the two-room model of heaven/earth relations mentioned earlier. The movie *Topper* reflects something like the first model where it is clearly understood that there is a second room beyond the first, and George and Marion consider it absolutely normal and totally appropriate that they should ascend to this second heavenly room. They are ready to go. Not so much because they yearn to meet their maker or anything like that, but because this is the normal, taken-for-granted thing that happens. You die, you go to heaven. No questions asked. Being a little absent-minded—because of their carefree life that wealth has bestowed upon them—they forget exactly what happens, but that's all. In their mind there is certainty over what should be done. It is their desire to do the appropriate thing, to find the key that will open the door to heaven and get them out of their in-between state as ghosts still attached to the here-and-now world of Cosmo Topper and his insufferable wife. George and Marion show no desire to cling to this world, even though they clearly enjoy themselves in it. They don't have regrets, hesitations, nor do they hesitate, question, resist, or try and bargain to stay earthbound; they are ready to go; they just need to find the "good deed key" to open that door and allow their ascent.

Ghost (1990)

Now fast forward to 1990 and the movie *Ghost,* which I have discussed earlier, but now want to look at in a slightly different light. This movie begins like *Topper* with an unexpected death taking the life of someone who had no idea that it was his time to go. There is also a similar loving couple, Sam (Patrick Swayze) and Molly (Demi Moore). This time only one of them dies—and reflecting social concerns fifty years later, Sam is killed by a mugger. Like George earlier, Sam leaves his body and does not believe that he is, in fact, a ghost. But like George and Marion he soon realizes his new condition.

If nothing had changed from our religious imagination that made *Topper* possible in 1937, the underlying assumption should still be the religious universe of the two-room model—the here and now and the eternity of an afterlife, with death as the doorway between them, and the certainty that one is supposed to pass from one to the other. In *Ghost* we have again reached the door of death, which means that life in the worldly room is now over and it is time to move on to the second room of eternity. George and Marion couldn't wait to find the "good deed key" to open the door and walk on through—"So long, Toppee, we're on our way." They were happy to go. They couldn't wait. And Sam? Is he wondering about how to get into heaven? Is he looking for that "good deed key" that will allow him to leave his ghostly status and ascend? It appears not, for in the first scene after he has taken spirit form, he is sitting on Molly's window sill resting his head on his knees, as a glum-faced, sad, depressed ghost without a clue as what to do next. It is the complete opposite of *Topper* where the ghosts' first thoughts were how to get out of their ghostly condition and get into heaven. But Sam doesn't want to go anywhere. He just sits there, pining away like a lovesick puppy watching Molly carry on in her apartment. Even as a spirit he just won't leave that first room, won't walk through that door and take his place in eternity. It turns out Sam will interfere in the events of Molly's life much like George and Marion did in Topper's life, but not to search for that "good deed key" to open heaven's door. No his good deed, if you want to call it that, is unexpectedly thrust in his lap when the mugger who killed him burgles Molly's apartment and threatens her life. This awakens him from his lovesick slumber and he goes into action protecting her, the ups and downs of which constitute the bulk of the movie. But when you think about it, if it weren't for the danger to Molly who knows how long Sam would have stayed there as a lovesick ghost, pining away in self pity, unwilling to ascend to heaven.

He eventually leaves his in-between state, but it's something of a reluctant parting. Having saved Molly and momentarily made contact through a kiss he still seems intent on staying where he is, or at least not leaving Molly's side, until Oda Mae (Whoopi Goldberg) the neighborhood channeler of spirits tells him, "They're waiting for you Sam." With that prod, he starts to back into the white light of the metaphoric heaven, looking back at Molly all the while. Backing into heaven while still looking at the things, creatures, feelings, of this world. Finally, saying "I love you Molly, I've always loved you" he turns and walks into the light. In *Topper* the ghosts couldn't wait to get to heaven. In *Ghost* the ghost is unsure exactly where he wants to be.

City of Angels (1998)

Now fast forward again to 1998 and the movie *City of Angels* based on the 1988 Wim Wenders film *Wings of Desire*. Think of *Topper's* George and Marion—spirit beings—sitting on a log talking about how to get into the other room, to use the metaphor introduced earlier. Now we have two more spirit beings (this time angels) sitting and talking. They, too, are wondering about the other room, except being already in heaven this means their discussion is about entering earthly life, rather than heavenly bliss. It is the reverse passage from *Topper*. George and Marion wanted to get into heaven. Now we see an angel named Seth wanting to get out of heaven. If we are used to seeing humans wonder what it would be like to be in heaven, we now have an angel wondering what it would be like to live as a mortal on earth.

The possibilities of the religious imagination have greatly expanded. In fact the direction of desire seems to have come full circle. In 1937 (*Topper*) the spirits desired to get into heaven. In 1990 (*Ghost*) the spirit couldn't decide whether he desired to get into heaven or not. In 1998 (*City of Angels*)[2] we see a spirit who desires to get out of heaven and into earthly form. Before considering what this might tell us about our religious imagination let's turn to some of the specifics of the movie.

Seth (Nicholas Cage) asks his angel companion Cassiel if he ever wondered what it would be like to experience "touch." He says no, which Seth doesn't believe, countering, "Yes you do!" Cassiel says ok, yes, occasionally he too wonders what it would be like to experience touch. In this movie the conversations are about going from one room to another, to use our metaphor, except now the contemplated transition is backward from eternity to contingent human form.

Seth the angel is a lot like Sam the ghost: a little on the mournful side, lonely, and somewhat uncertain as to what he wants and it turns out, deeply in love with Maggie, a surgeon he sees in a hospital. While losing a patient on the operating table she seems to look right at him. Seth later asks Cassiel, "Have you ever been seen like you were a man?" "She can't see you unless you want her to," he replies, and now we realize that it is his desire for her to see him. The direction of spiritual desire is now reversed. The effort is now to get to earth from heaven. The angel has fallen in love with the mortal and follows her everywhere: sneaking up behind Maggie to smell her hair, watching her take a bath, and watching her fight with her boyfriend, only to retire to the bedroom to make love. Seth watches them go, dejected like a victim without any control over the situation. The girl he loves is going into the bedroom to, make love to another man. The angst on his face. An angel in angst. Occasionally he lets her see him and they talk. After a few such meetings she falls in love with him too. It's that look of desire and regret about being in a spiritual, rather than mortal form, that also appeared on Sam's face in *Ghost*.

There is an obvious problem: he is an angel and she is mortal. How are their desires to be resolved. The answer comes through a hospital patient Seth meets called Nathan Messinger, played by Dennis Franz, who takes Peter Falk's role in the earlier *Wings of Desire*. It turns out Nathan is a fallen angel himself, and as he stuffs food into his mouth at a diner sitting across from Seth he introduces himself as a hedonist and glutton—"former celestial body, recent addition to the human race." He goes on to explain to Seth that God gave free will not only to mankind but to angels too, so, "you choose to fall to earth. Just make up your mind to do it." Seth then asks Nathan why he fell to earth. As he pulls some pictures from his wallet he starts in, "My daughter Ruth, her stupid husband Frank" and the grandkids, his wife, and so on. It's a wonderful touch. What in another movie is a complaint about the burdens of an extended family, the wife, kids, stupid son-in-law, etc. is here a reason to give up a heavenly existence. High praise for daily life. In this sense this movie is also a reminder of the taken-for-granted wonder of ordinary existence— touch, warmth, biting into a juicy pear, smelling a woman's freshly washed hair, having a spouse, kids, and in-laws. In an odd sort of way—although maybe that was the point of this movie – the real angelic thing Seth does is to remind all of us about the glories of our human existence. When you think about it there is no higher praise of human existence than for someone to give up perfection and eternity to join the human race for a limited number of years knowing that death, perhaps drawn out and painful, is what awaits.

Nathan now asks if the angels still gather on the beach at dawn to hear celestial music. Seth says yes and so they go to the beach. Nathan closes his eyes and tries to hear the music and can't. "No, I can't hear that, but you can't feel this," he says and proceeds to take his clothes off and run into the California surf to catch a wave. What a contrast with the angels on the beach, standing there supposedly in heavenly bliss, yet seeming more like bloodless zombies frozen in time and stuck into the sand like Easter Island statuary, and the life-affirming Rubenesque figure of Nathan waving his arms as he joyously jumps into the water. What's really joyous and heavenly and what's not? Given the options presented here, who wouldn't want to fall to earth.

Seth now explains this "falling to earth" possibility to Cassiel—you just make up your mind to do it, you just fall. Then you can smell the air, taste the water, read a newspaper, lie—through the teeth—feed the dog, touch her hair. Cassiel listens and it must all sound pretty good to him too, for he doesn't try and talk Seth out of anything. All he says is, "What are you waiting for." "There is so much beauty up here," says Seth, as if weighing the advantages of heaven vs. his desire for the sensations of earth. But it isn't much of a choice, what with the angels being dressed, standing around very non-emotional, watching life in a very passive way. It turns out Seth doesn't think there is much of a choice either, and you just know he is going to take the plunge and he does, taking a swan dive off a building and awakening on the ground, with bruised and bloodied hands and a cut lip, but, most important, fully human.

He now goes to find Maggie at a cabin on Lake Tahoe. The result: all he desired. Love. Union. Happiness. In the original movie the angel who falls ends up living with a trapeze artist. Here, for whatever reason, Maggie is hit by a truck returning with some breakfast groceries the next morning. Seth runs to her side. She whispers, "I wanted to show you everything. I am sorry," but he disagrees, and tells her that "to touch you, to feel you, to hold you right now, do you know how much I love you?" Was it worth it? Giving up eternity in heaven for these few moments of love? Cassiel asks Seth, "If you knew this was going to happen would you have done it?" Seth: "I would rather of had one breath of her hair, one kiss of her mouth, one touch of her hand, than eternity without it..." There is the answer: preferring one touch, one breath, one kiss to eternal bliss.

Final scene. Back on the beach. All the angels, dressed in those black trench coats, standing there stiff as boards listening to their celestial sounds, and now Seth, like Nathan before, stands there too, trying to hear the music. But he is no longer an angel, and he too breaks for the beach and plunges into the surf. Cassiel watches. His stoic face now breaks into a huge smile, clearly happy about Seth's choice. Here we see not only the glory of being alive (plunging into the exhilarating cold water of the ocean) but the seeming approval by heaven of that choice.

Cassiel seems so happy that you could imagine that someday he would take the plunge and fall to earth, and I suppose another angel would smilingly approve, and if she then fell to earth, her friend would smilingly approve, and if she fell, well, pretty soon there wouldn't be any angels left in heaven. I realize this is a perhaps unwarranted conclusion, but consider what we have been presented with: life in heaven where the angels don't seem particularly happy and mope around much of the time dressed in flat black, rarely smiling, and almost never laughing. This dress and demeanor makes heaven seem like East Berlin under Communism—lifeless, grey, and depressing. From this point of view, no wonder angels want to jump over this Berlin Wall between heaven and earth.[3] And it's not just Seth who misses earth. He was going to make a decorative pair of angel wings for a little girl who died on the operating table whom he had escorted to heaven. But she tells him, "What good would wings be if you couldn't feel the wind on your face." She has, in theory, everything—which is what heaven is supposed to mean—yet, it is not enough. She misses the wind on her face.

Now, what does all this tell us about the religious imagination? First, there is the noticeable shift in desires from wanting to get into heaven, to being unsure, to wanting to leave heaven. What does this mean for the evolution of the religious imagination? Perhaps nothing, for other contemporary movies with angels show no signs of serious angel angst. Denzel Washington, the angel in *The Preachers Wife*, is there only to help and shows no desire to stay earthside, and John Travolta's angel in *Michael* may be a hard-drinking, fist-fighting, carousing fellow, but all that is in the service of coming to the aid of a mortal in need. No, Seth's angel angst seems pretty much his own, and considering the original idea of an angel in angst came from the German movie *Wings of Desire*, what we may have here is a reading of some more traditional German angst into the character of Seth the angel.

But that, of course, makes the very point of our book: depicting religious subjects is of necessity a work of the human imagination. There is simply no real, accurate, actual, literal, or concrete picture of angels, so there is no choice but to construct an image and that opens the door to all sorts of cultural, historical, and denominational influences. It is, then, no wonder that we read contemporary psychology into angel personalities. If humans have angst, they can see angel angst; if humans are endowed with free will, so should angels be, and if it is a sign of authenticity not only to be in touch with one's feelings but to honestly act upon them, then it is only a matter of time before the picturing of angels is in the form of Seth and his existential crisis.

In that regard Aries noted how there has been a gradual individuation of death corresponding to the rise of individualism in economic and political life. From writing wills to the appearance of a single marker for each grave, the rituals of death increasingly articulate the presence of the unique individual.[4] From what we have seen in the shift from *Topper* through *Ghost* to *City of Angels* there also seems to be an increase in the central role of the discrete self (including, most interestingly, the ghost and angel self) as the touchstone of decision making. Angels as well as mortals, not only have free will it appears, but place an importance on being in touch with one's feelings. Seth the angel fell in love; his feelings took control, and he honored those feelings, even at the expense of his heavenly duties. The anthropologists might have said Seth went native, but there was no judgment by the other angels of his choice — if anything from what we saw of Cassiel's reaction, he was completely in favor of the fall. Seth's making overtures to, then falling in love with, then leaving to join Maggie was not judged at all. His flirtatious overtures to Maggie were not condemned by the other angels. It was not seen by the angelic community as a question of something like a doctor sleeping with a patient, nor did anyone raise the question of whether he had an obligation to stay in heaven. Cassiel never asked Seth if he ever wondered what the boss would say about this "falling to earth" business. No, Seth was more an independent agent, almost as though being an angel was a role he played working for heaven, and when he decided he wanted to change "jobs" he felt free to do so.

Is this-worldly life being elevated above a possible heavenly afterlife? Perhaps that was the intent of the filmmakers. It certainly was a ringing endorsement of the wonders of being alive. But it is also a testament to the continued flexibility of the religious imagination. We have seen, and accepted, bird wings attached to human backs as a representation of an angel. No one considers that sacrilegious. Now we have an angel with a mind of his own, who it also turns out makes a rather surprising decision with that free will. It has been said that people get the government they deserve. I suppose the same holds for their religious imagination. We get the pictures of angels that we deserve. We are a society that believes in free decision making and authentic relationships. Why should that be kept only for ourselves. There is no reason why it will not seep into our religious imagination, and from the certainty of George and Marion through the indecision of Sam to the angst and free decision to leave heaven of Seth, we have seen the autonomy of ghosts and angels only increase.

A.J.B.

Notes

1. *I Married an Angel* (1942), *It's a Wonderful Life* (1946), *The Bishop's Wife* (1947), *Heaven Only Knows* (1947), *Angels in the Outfield* (1951), *The Heavenly Kid* (1985), *Date with an Angel* (1987), *Wings of Desire* (1987), *Almost an Angel* (1990), *So Faraway, So Close!* (1993), *Angels in*

the Outfield (1994), *The Prophecy* (1995), *Michael* (1996), *The Preacher's Wife* (1996), *A Life Less Ordinary* (1997), *City of Angels* (1998), *The Prophecy II* (1998).

2. I realize this 1998 movie is a remake of one made in 1988.

3. Actually the original, *Wings of Desire*, was set in Berlin and the angels dressed in wintry coats, which for wet, blustery, cold northern Germany made some sense. Why that motif was continued when the angels shifted to sunny California escapes me.

4. For instance around the fifth century CE inscriptions and portraits disappeared from tombs, which some have attributed to the decline of writing in general. Then, after the twelfth century, and first among the rich and powerful, the attitude of funeral anonymity began to decline. The first inscriptions on head stones centered on the name of the deceased, and by the fourteenth and fifteenth centuries date of birth and age appeared, and by the sixteenth and seventeenth centuries more personal biography was sketched in (here lies John Smith married to...), and exceptional events in one's life, like military honors and citations. During these same centuries, between the fifteenth and early nineteenth, the symbol of the cross as the simple marker of the individual grave gradually became institutionalized.

12

A Note on Purgatory in the Movies

Greeley's First Law: When other people discover something, Catholics are busy trying to forget it. They discover Purgatory while, with shamed faces, we try to pretend that the Purgatory tradition really isn't there. Purgatory—not named as such—appears in the movies and we ignore the history—and the grace—of the Purgatory story.[1]

One can find on the worldwide web fifteen neatly grouped Catholic articles on Purgatory. All of them could have been written before the Second Vatican Council, all of them pretend that the Church has taught Purgatory from the beginning, all of them ignore the historical fact that Purgatory first came into the Catholic heritage (as a place) in the early Middle Ages. The term was first used in print by a monk who dubbed himself as "H" from the English monastery of Salton. He recorded the tale of "St. Patrick's Purgatory" on Station Island in Lough Derg in Ireland. (Still a place of pilgrimage and visited more recently by the Nobel laureate Seamus Heaney in a collection of his poems called *Station Island*.)

The belief that prayers for the dead are appropriate goes back to the Maccabees who sent offerings up to Jerusalem because "it is a holy and wholesome thought to pray for the dead that they might be loosed from their sins." Christianity absorbed the custom and the belief. There has always been a belief of some sort in an intermediate state between death and paradise. Catholicism, for all its romance with scholastic philosophy, loves the concrete. Therefore in the Middle Ages it made the state a place and gave it a name—*Purgatorium*, a place of purification. Dante made it famous with his vivid pictures of suffering souls being purged of the remnants of their sins before their admission into heaven. Luther rejected the idea because in his perspective God's loving mercy forgave

119

everything, hence a Purgatory was not necessary. In the Catholic tradition one need not believe that Purgatory is a place (only a state) or that there is physical suffering in it (no fire!). In the years since the Second Vatican Council, Catholic theologians have paid little attention to Purgatory, perhaps because, like the Mother of Jesus, it is considered an ecumenical encumbrance.

The Catholic laity continue to pray for and to the "souls in Purgatory," ignoring as they usually do, the fads and fashions of their theologians.

The problem with the traditional teaching on Purgatory is that it is essentially legalist. People commit sins. They confess their sins and promise to try not to commit them again. However, they still bear guilt for the harm done by them. This is only "temporal" guilt but it must be expiated before they can enjoy eternal happiness, either by good works or indulgences or suffering in Purgatory. In the confusion and chaos of the collapse of the Roman Empire and the rebuilding of Europe, law, punishment, guilt, expiation were deemed to be a sufficient response to human propensities to do wrong. Although St. Augustine and even St. Paul had introduced the notion of the subjective into religious discourse and although the moral theologians in later centuries accepted the notion that moral responsibility could be diminished in various ways by subjective factors, a sense of intra- and inter-subjectivity would have to wait till the Renaissance (if we accept Harold Bloom's theory on Shakespeare) and even to the post-Freudian world.

I am not suggesting that only we moderns reflect on our own consciousness or that no one before us has been able to imagine another person as a "thou." More modestly I propose that we have the vocabulary, the time, and the leisure to think about ourselves and about our various intimate others. Regrets over the failure to make the most of our personal resources have become an explicit issue on the human agenda only recently. Failures in relationships with others, perceived however dimly as other "selves" have become an explicit subject of personal concern only a short while ago as human history goes. Thus in *Flatliners*, how the medical students deal with both issues becomes the explicit theme of the movie. They have failed themselves. They have failed those they love or should love. They must make reparation. They must expiate. No longer would it be enough to go off to a monastery (or a convent) for the rest of their lives, or win an indulgence by making a grant to the construction of St. Peter's, or sign up for a Crusade. Now we must make amends to ourselves and to others by some modification of the self. Prayer and fasting are no longer adequate atonement. More-over, these issues fill contemporary literature and have become part of the atmosphere and ambience of our lives. We can hardly think about ourselves and our lives for more than fifteen minutes without realizing how much we have wasted both of our own resources and of the possi-bilities in our relationships with one another. "Expiate! Expiate!" as the J. D. Salinger character said.

Not everyone by any means takes seriously the responsibility to ex-piate, or more precisely to somehow make up for all the lost opportuni-ties. Enough of us do, however, to realize that we will never regain those lost opportunities and the best we can expect is that in whatever years of life we have ahead of us we may not waste so many.

I suggest that Purgatory-like themes appear in many of the movies about God, because there is a dim but powerful human longing for a chance, not exactly to expiate, but straighten things out. If God wants something back on his investment in giving us life, perhaps He will give us another chance to straighten out the mess we have made of it. The filmmakers probably do not know from Purgatory, but they do un-derstand regret and the longing for a second chance. They may also sense that if there is to be a final second chance it will require some special intervention from someone who is powerful enough to grant such a second chance. God may well be invoked by many filmmakers, precisely because their story-line, their creative imagination requires that characters get a second chance.

Viewed from this perspective, many of the films we have discussed involve second chances (Purgatory-like experiences) because, however unwittingly, the filmmakers are aware of this human need in a world where our species has become much more explicit about the intra-sub-jective and the inter-subjective.

The most powerful recent writing on Purgatory is in the novel *The White Hotel* by the Cornish writer D. M. Thomas. In the "Coda" of this powerful book he depicts the Holocaust martyrs arriving in "transports" from the gas chambers in a kind of Israel, that is something like the contemporary state of Israel, but obviously very different. With allu-sions to *The Divine Comedy* he suggests that it is a place of physical and spiritual preparation for entrance into the *Paradiso*. The principle spiritual task is straightening out the relationships which a person has bungled during life. Apparently one need not make them perfect, only arrive at the beginning of an understanding. In this perspective Purgatory is an antechamber of heaven, perhaps even a part of it, where we try to undo the messes we have made in our lives.

This notion of reworking relationships expands the "remission of the temporal punishment due to sin," a theological construct developed by more legalistic Catholic writers. What remains of our sins even after they have been forgiven? The harm done to other people, the shattered relationships, the hurt feelings, the rejection of love and indeed the harm done to ourselves by our failure to treat others as "thou." Catholic theologians ignored Thomas, though his idea seemed utterly orthodox, however wild his metaphors. It makes sense that humans be given an opportunity to work their way through the unfinished agenda of their lives. Reconciliation is both difficult and pleasant, hard work and enjoyable, embarrassing and deeply rewarding. Purgatory is a grace.

Some day Catholic theologians will catch up with D. M. Thomas and with the filmmakers for whom an intermediate situation is an appropriate, perhaps necessary, plot device. None of them call it Purgatory. They might not even realize that the intermediate situation is like Purgatory. Yet they do suggest that there is unfinished business after death which the dead can and perhaps must deal with. Perhaps the filmmakers understand that there is a strong propensity in humankind to attempt to cancel out regrets by seeking and receiving forgiveness. Perhaps they also understand, as did the ancient Celts, the human need to believe that the dead are not far away at all. Finally, it is just possible that they may intuit the notion that the generous and forgiving God whom they present in their films almost has to grant humans an intermediate situation where they can straighten out some of the worst messes of their lives.

Thomas's characters, incidentally, rehabilitate their relationships with gentleness and delicacy. Their reconciliations are not maudlin and do not focus on who was guilty of what. Nor do they have an agenda of charges and complaints and counter-charges and counter-complaints. Rather they engage in sensitive quests for understanding, perhaps like a reconciliation between married lovers, who in their confidence that this quarrel is over and will not recur, now seek for further insight into one another, perhaps as they prepare to seal their renewal of love with an act of love.

Small wonder that the Celts, who believed that boundaries between the living and the dead are thin, called the lands of promise in the West, "the many-colored lands." If Purgatory is like that (and I believe that it is) then it sounds like a fun place and I look forward to it.

Thus in *Field of Dreams*, the "Black Sox" must come back to discharge their obligations to the fans. This generosity wins for them a new opportunity. In *Always* Audrey Hepburn tells Richard Dreyfuss that his work is finished only when he passes on his skills to another pilot. Dreyfuss must relinquish his possessive relationship with the woman he loves. In *Flatliners*, the young medical students are given an opportunity while they are at the edge of death to give and receive forgiveness from those they have harmed. In *Jacob's Ladder*, Jacob Singer must make his peace with someone, though who that someone is depends on how you choose to interpret the film. In *Ghost* Patrick Swayze must break the barriers of death to protect his beloved from a dangerous criminal. In *Truly, Madly, Deeply*, Jamie has to come back from the dead (with his band of musicians) to release his beloved from the prison of grief she has built around herself, perhaps because of the imperfections which he had created in their relationship. In *All That Jazz*, Joe Gideon has a chance to say that he's sorry. In *The Rapture* the woman is given a chance after death to accept (as it seems to us) the unfair demand of a fundamentalist God. In a certain sense even the Eucharist-like feast which Babette prepares can be considered as a reconciliation which occurs but rarely in this life and perhaps as an anticipation of Purgatory. Perhaps there are many festivals in Purgatory in which we sit around a table with those we love and clean away the horror of misunderstandings and hidden agenda so that we may move permanently with them into reconciled love.

The Purgatory sequences in the movies about God are indeed opportunities for love to be reestablished and for lovers to be permanently reconciled, festivals of forgiveness and understanding made possible by a God who is pure forgiveness.

It is as if the filmmakers perceive that if they are trying to cope with the meaning of life and death—and hence God must be invoked in some guise or other—they need a time between life and death when the final confusions of life may be worked out. They are driven to creating Purgatory-like situations, not because of theological assumptions, but because they can't do without it.

Does this mean that there is in fact a Purgatory-like situation or even a Purgatory place where forgiveness and reconciliation are the work, the harsh and sweet work, that needs to be done?

Neither the sociologist nor the filmmaker knows the answer to that question. The filmmaker knows that such an assumption fits the demands of his plot structure. The sociologist knows that it is a graceful assumption which is bound to appeal to both audiences and congregations.

Are the boundaries between the living and the dead as thin as *Flatliners* (in agreement with the Celts) seems to suggest? Perhaps, it would be nice if they were. It would be nice if there were a Purgatory. It would be nice if love can be renewed after death, and forgiveness both received and bestowed. It would be nice if we could recapture the missed opportunities for reconciliation in our life. That it would be nice doesn't prove that it is so, but it doesn't prove that it isn't either.

Why must we wait till we are dead to reconcile? Why not make peace with everyone (parents, children, lovers, spouses, friends) while we're still alive and enjoy that peace both in this life and in the Land of Promise?

Why not, indeed?

In D. M. Thomas's Purgatory, the protagonist and her mother and father reconcile with surprising ease. It seems that they have lost their fear of one another (as, for example, do many of the young medical students in *Flatliners*). Perhaps in Purgatory God grants special strength for the delightful and difficult task of reconciliation. Or perhaps, after you're dead, there is nothing more to fear. Maybe our conflicts and quarrels are mostly the result of fear which ultimately is the fear of death. Maybe it will be easy to love one another the way we want to after we are dead, because that fear now is absurd.

Maybe God wants to burnish us and polish us and spiff us up so that we enter into our permanent joy as fresh as a lad on his First Communion Day, as a bride on her wedding day, as a mother at the baptism of her first child, as a college grad with a brand new diploma on graduation day.

I find myself thinking that I hope so and then understanding that Purgatory in the movies is about hope.

A.M.G

Note

1. The Second Law is like the first: when Catholics discover something, everyone else is abandoning it. The third is that the willingness of a religious institution to tell secular institutions how to solve their problems is in inverse relationship to the ability of that institution to solve its own problems.

13

How to Put God in a Movie

My co-author has argued that religion arises from experiences of grace, where something happens in human affairs that cannot be attributed to the normal workings of the world, hence suggesting the presence of a larger and more purposeful presence, like God. Such grace experiences, which are sprinkled throughout life, are captured in symbols and passed down through the generations in story form, which would now include movies. So far we have focused largely upon the wide variety of symbols used to dramatize this religious imagination, from bright white light (*Fearless*) and chiropractors (*Jacob's Ladder*) to beautiful women (*Always, All That Jazz*) and little old men (*Oh, God!*). This screening of symbols of grace, from angels to heaven to God seems easy enough. But the process is more complicated, for not every kind of movie is comfortable with hints of God's presence. To explore this issue I want to discuss two general kinds of movies, what I will call the micro realist and the macro science fiction movie.

The Micro-Realist Movie

First, let's ask the question of why we don't see hints of God's presence in many movies. The simplest answer is that this is not a point the filmmaker wishes to make; some sort of divine intervention just doesn't fit into the narrative. That's probably the most common reason and makes the most sense. But we can unpack this idea a little. Movies that are considered serious in the sense of trying to make a comment on the human condition invariable set themselves in a very naturalistic or realistic setting. The idea is to portray emotions, feelings, anger, love,

125

and loss as they really occur and not avoid the unpleasant or smooth over the harsh realities of life. We can calls these "micro" movies because their central point centers on interpersonal relations or the psychological dynamics of their characters. The micro movie gains much of its power from this depiction of human life as it really happens; no punches are pulled and no contrived endings are allowed. It is as it is, or as the filmmaker thinks it is. In this regard, what Tom Wolfe said about the realism of the novel also seems applicable to the realism of the micro movie: "It was realism that created the 'absorbing' or 'gripping' quality that is peculiar to the novel, the quality that makes the reader feel that he has been pulled not only into the setting of the story but also into the minds....of the characters."[1] Even blockbuster action adventure movies flooded with special effects have a commitment to realism as they try to represent things like terrorist attacks, runaway trains, sinking ships, hijacked airplanes, or volcanic explosions, realistically, as if you were really there. The emphasis on reality here is ratcheted up to a realistic depiction of the historical event or action-adventure rather than ratcheted down to the human emotion. Some movies, manage a naturalism of setting and human response. *Lawrence of Arabia* is both the spectacle of the Arab revolt during World War I and a personal tragedy. The *Godfather* is both an historical drama and the personal story of the tragic price a son pays to follow in his father's footsteps in the family business.

Such an emphasis upon life-as-it-is-realism as a story's backdrop has direct implications for placing hints of God on the screen, for supernatural intrusions violate the integrity of daily reality, hence the integrity of the very realistic story being told. As a result most movies with a realistic or naturalistic commitment—from serious micro explorations of the human condition to historical dramas or special effects action-adventure spectaculars—do not attempt to portray unexplainable intrusions that their characters acknowledge as grace experiences. For instance, the film magazine *Time Out*[2] conducted a readers' poll of the top 100 movies. *It's a Wonderful Life*, with the appearance of Clarence the angel and Wim Wenders *Wings of Desire* about the angel who falls to earth, seemed the only God in the movies movies on their list. Similarly, in 1998 the American Film Institute had a distinguished panel select the 100 greatest American movies, and only *It's A Wonderful Life* and *Star Wars* (if the "force" is seen as a metaphor for something like God) seemed like the movies we discuss here. The AFI top one hundred starts out with *Citizen Kane, Casablanca, The Godfather, Gone with the Wind, Lawrence of Arabia, The Wizard of Oz, The Graduate, On the Waterfront, Schindler's List, Singin' in the Rain,* and closes with *My Fair Lady, A Place in the Sun, The Apartment, Goodfellas, Pulp Fiction, The Searchers, Bringing up Baby, Unforgiven, Guess Who's Coming to Dinner,* and *Yankee Doodle Dandy.* Some of them are about the present, some about the past, some made up, but most are based on a world devoid of hints of a divine presence. Realistic movies can be about religion, but mostly where we see human reactions to playing roles in religious organizations (stories about priests, nuns, rabbis, ministers, televangelists), or holding religious beliefs (consequences of accepting faith, losing faith, bigotry, helpfulness, kindness), or about religious organizations in historical context (*Ben Hur, The Big Fisherman*). But these religious movies are about human nature (as a natural entity) reacting to religious beliefs and institutions, and not an effort at an actual screening of a hint of God's presence.

The Macro-Sci Fi Movie

If it is difficult to have hints of the supernatural intrude into films with a deep commitment to a believable everyday reality, then it would seem the more open-ended, everything is possible science fiction movie would constitute a much better backdrop for hints about God's presence. But this isn't so either, although for different reasons. If, in the micro human story movie, everyday reality is just too tight to allow a hint of God to peek through, then the open-ended science fiction is just too loose. In these futuristic worlds anything goes and nothing is impossible. Where reality ends and the supernatural begins is never pinned down, making it extremely difficult to come to the conclusion that something is ever from the other side. How can anyone suspect God when it might be some alien force or some parallel universe or some cosmic space time warp?

Science fiction movies do, though, have a great deal of extraworldly intrusions that are not found in micro realist movies, which could, in principle, be taken for hints of God's presence. But by and large, they aren't, because it is always possible that there is some natural thing out there that is the cause. What science fiction does, then, is to naturalize extra ordinary occurrences, turning potential grace experiences into science-like puzzles, where the normal reaction is to search for a solution rather than be awestruck and suspect the presence of the divine. No matter how out of the world the initial premise, the rest of the movie turns into a technical game of figuring out how this extraordinary experience is, in fact, part of the laws of some physics somewhere. Even when the characters don't know the exact science of what is going on, the conclusion isn't that this is a hint of God's presence, but that this is simply a world so advanced that we as yet don't understand its operating principles.

Oh, God!

To get a feel for this naturalizing effect consider the culminating scene in the non-science fiction movie, *Oh, God!,* where George Burns is in court claiming to be God. Now imagine this same scene in, say, a *Star Trek* movie. In *Oh, God!* no one believes Burns is really God and so he proposes a small demonstration. He starts to walk out of the courtroom. Halfway out he turns invisible, then continues to walk out, pushing—without being seen—the doors open at the end of the courtroom to enter the hallway. Here we have a clear commitment to everyday reality—a day in court in southern California—and a very unnatural, if not downright supernatural, event, turning invisible. The reaction of everyone in the courthouse is shock and amazement. Mouths drop open. They stare in disbelief. They can't believe what they have just seen. It brings the whole scene to a halt. Now, replay this scene as if on board the Starship Enterprise. George Burns starts to walk down the aisle and turns invisible. What is the reaction of Captain Piccard, or Captain Kirk? Is it amazement, awe, and the sense on their face that they have just witnessed a possible presence of the divine? Probably not. My guess is that they would say something to the effect, "Damn, its those Klingons again and their 'cloaking device.' They have obviously perfected it to be used on people as well as space ships." And if it wasn't the Klingons it would be some other beings from some planet in some parallel universe. All the things George Burns (God) did to John Denver in *Oh, God!,* from appearing out of thin air, to making it rain inside his car, to making sounds appear out of nowhere, and creating the presence of, or illusion of, upper floors of an office building, would all be seen to be special powers of some alien creatures or some different physics of some different universe. The point is it's always something. The extraordinary is never unexplainable. Therefore it is never an act of grace.

And that's the key point of why science fiction is not compatible with screening hints of God's presence.

2001: A Space Odyssey

The difficulty of creating a sense of awe in science fiction can be seen in the movie *2001: A Space Odyssey* which has often been described as having spiritual and religious overtones. This movie is deeply committed to science fiction. It will take something impossible and make it seem possible, from the presence of a black monolith stuck into the surface of the moon, through the exploratory space journey to Jupiter to see where a mysterious signal is coming from. Even the computer that malfunctions, Hal, is believable as what computers might be like in the future. In the end the movie could easily be said to be spiritual or religious, but the characters on the screen give no hint that they are in the presence of something divine or unaccountable.

Dave Bowman (Keir Dullea) the last living person on the space ship, finally leaves the mother ship and heads off in his pod toward Jupiter and another monolith we see floating in space. Before considering Dave's reaction to this, shift back to *Oh, God!* for a moment. Remember John Denver's expression when he discovers the extraordinary things George Burns can, and does, do. He is shaken to the core and can't believe what he is seeing. Experiencing rain just inside his car, someone who turns invisible and appears and disappears at will, all throw him for a loop. He breaks down and quivers in his bathroom when George Burns appears. And Dave? When he sees and experiences extraordinary things, does he react in the same normal way he had throughout the movie? Is he shook up, surprised, startled, or fearful to find hunks of metal in space or that he is being transported through a light show reminiscent of a Haight-Ashbury tunnel of visual delights? It doesn't seem like it, or if he is, we would never know. He just keeps going in his pod. You never hear him say to himself, "Oh my God, look at those colors, what the hell is going on here, where the hell am I?" And when his pod finally lands, he is in some eighteenth-century rococo drawing room where, looking out the pod window, he sees himself walking across the room to see someone else sitting down eating at a table. Does he say, "What is going on here; this is crazy, am I dreaming, on drugs, what?" No, not at all. Well, it gets even crazier as the guy at the table, turns out to be an older Dave, who now gets up and sees someone in bed, and its

Dave even older yet, and as this dying old man reaches for the monolith, now at the end of his bed his body is transformed into a glowing fetus.

I understand all of this is supposed to be poetic imagery. And it is. But that is my very point. To attain something extraordinary, hence to hint at something spiritual or religious, requires violating the integrity of the science fiction premise upon which *2001* was built. Up until Dave departed the mother ship, everything seemed quite natural. The monolith discovered on the moon is treated as if it is really there. Haywood Floyd the space scientist flies out to take a look. Great care is taken to make it all seem realistic. He dozes on the flight and his pen floats in the weightlessness of space; he calls his daughter and wishes her a happy birthday on the moon colony's pay phone; and he casually opens a box lunch and has a sandwich as the space shuttle scoots across the moon's surface heading toward the implanted monolith. This is followed by the exacting reality of the space flight to Jupiter. Hal, the talking computer of the future, seems real. Dave's reactions also seem real: he is co-piloting the mission, he logically figures out a way to get back on the ship after Hal locks him out; and he reasonably decides its time to disconnect Hal. All normal reactions.

What, then, is one to make of Dave's decision to get into his pod and head out alone for Jupiter and that flying piece of monolithic metal? Suicide? That doesn't seem part of the spiritual message this ending is supposed to convey. But if we stick with the science fiction premise so far, there are few other reasonable conclusions. Going off alone is certain death, so why does he do it? There isn't an answer, of course, and that is part of the eternal mystery of this movie. Some say it is supposed to make us think and speculate or that the images that follow are trying to hint at things like human evolution or cosmic rebirth. All of which is fine and these images succeed, more or less, in placing such hints. But what must be recognized is that this effort at the larger cosmic, or religious implication, is only attainable by rupturing the science fiction premise upon which the movie is founded. Why is the science fiction abandoned? Who knows, but let me suggest that the openness of the science fiction format, in naturalizing everything in its path, now leaves no room at the end of the movie for the intended spiritual, mystical, religious, or cosmic conclusion that is desired.

If the science fiction premise continued, and there was an extraordinary intrusion, whether the floating monolith or the chateau-like room in space, Dave, following the science fiction premise, would be compelled to treat it as a real problem and try and figure out a solution. After all this is what happened when they found the monolith on the moon. No one said this might be some sort of divine signal. They went to investigate as if it were a natural phenomena. And the signal from Jupiter. They went to investigate that too. And Hal's malfunction, it too was treated in a normal rational fashion: disconnect the computer. But now Dave, at movie's end, doesn't treat his new experiences in this way at all. He seems spellbound by the light show and undisturbed to find someone like himself in this rococo room. The reason, of course, is that Dave is no longer Dave the real space man, but now Dave the cut-out image assembled along with a marble floored eighteenth-century room, the dying old man, and the glowing fetus to create a montage of images that works better as a painting than as a continuation of the science fiction narrative that made up most of the movie.

In short, the movie was stuck. It wanted to make a larger spiritual message but the science fiction format would have absorbed any such outrageous thing it could possibly come up with, so it just switched to being a collage of images. *2001: The Science Fiction Movie* ended when Dave left the pod on his own and *2001: The Collage* art work began.

It is as if Kubrick decided at the end to turn the movie into a painting because he couldn't introduce his spiritual/religious message about human birth/re-birth within the format that had gotten Dave and the spaceship close to Jupiter. The movie screen became a giant collage. In 1914 Georges Braque assembled a collage titled "Newspaper, Bottle, Packet of Tobacco" and in 1968 Stanley Kubrick ended his space movie with a silver screen collage we could call, "Rococo Dining Room, Old Man Eating/Dying, Glowing Fetus."

I think there was no choice, given the science fiction premise. The passive aggressiveness of science fiction would have absorbed any effort at hints of the extraordinary and without his collage at the end he would have been left with *Star Trek* or *Star Wars*, or any other science fiction movie. The only way out of science fiction reality is to end the movie and start a painting within the movie. Did his collage work? The film is loved, but the ending has remained controversial on the simple grounds that no one seems to know what it really means. I believe that a good part of this comes from abandoning his science fiction medium to insert his collage construction.

Star Wars

I mentioned *Star Wars* earlier, and certainly the notion of the "Force" seems like a real metaphor for something like God. Vaya con dios, "May the force be with you," certainly hints at this. But the naturalizing effect of science fiction can be seen here too, as the Force seems a natural entity. Compare, for example, the *Star Wars* Force with the *Field of Dreams* Voice. Both seem supernatural on the surface, but upon closer examination the Force appears more natural. Everyone seems to agree that the Force exists, and that some have it and some don't. Compared to the mystery of the Voice in *Field of Dreams* the "Force" seems more like magnetism, a natural entity to be harnessed for human purposes. Luke Skywalker also isn't that surprised, confused, or in doubt over the presence of the Force in anyway comparable to Ray Kinsella being startled, unclear, unsure, and something in awe when the Voice talks to him. When, for instance, the voice of the deceased Jedi knight Obi-wan Kenobi starts to talk to Luke in the cockpit of his fighter plane while attacking the Death Star, Luke says something to this effect, "Obi-wan is that you," as if communication with the astral plane is a normal state of affairs. Luke does not say, "What is this, a ghost, I thought you were dead; who are you; what do you want, why are you talking to me," in the surprised and angry tones used by Ray Kinsella when addressed by the Voice. In the *Star Wars* world, with their special physics, such things seem very possible, and so Luke just heeds the voice's advice about relying on the Force rather than his instrument panel to attack the Death Star. When advised "If you build it, he will come," Ray Kinsella doesn't say, in a familiar voice, "'Voice,' is that you," for in his cosmos there is no such possibility. The *Star Wars* Force, though, isn't so much from the other side, as a functioning element somewhere in a science fiction cosmos. Anything is possible, including the power of the Force. This flexibility neuters the sense of the truly extraordinary and keeps those events from having a grace-like interpretation.

In this regard consider the character of Yoda. Is he a mystery? Not at all. He is just there, this guy with these mysterious powers, that we all believe exist somewhere in the future. Luke is certainly calm about it all. He just wants his lessons. No puzzlement here. I suppose the closest thing we have to a portrayal of something like heaven comes at the end of *Return of the Jedi* when we see the spirit beings of Darth Vader, Yoda, and Obi-wan Kenobi watching Luke and the others celebrate. I think Luke looks at them and smiles; they look back and smile. A normal day out here in deep space where life on the astral plane is part of normal physics, such that no one is surprised that the deceased should materialize in front of everyone, or that you should recognize their presence. Compare this with the looks of Molly and Sam at the end of *Ghost*. Molly is amazed that she can see Sam and the emotion is overwhelming that spirt has become if not flesh, then at least visually materialized in some capacity. Agreed, they were husband and wife and that accounts for a lot of the emotion, but the possibility of a crossing between the living and dead was also a tremendous emotional experience for both of them.

Micro + Macro = A Hint of the Divine

If we eliminate the macro science fiction movie too, how then does one put a hint of God in a movie? There are no doubt many ways, but here is one. If micro films portray a reality so tightly drawn it doesn't allow for intrusions from the other side, and if the macro science fiction films provide cosmic intrusions, but naturalize them, then what is the correct cinematic formula? The answer is to combine the strength of each genre. From the science fiction movie take the presence of unexplainable intrusions into everyday reality, but now insert them into the tightly defined reality of the micro realist movie. The result: things we can't explain plus the awe and amazement produced by the fact that this event cannot be explained in worldly terms, leaving a hint of God as the only other possibility. Both elements are absolutely necessary. It cannot work with only one or the other. In science fiction things happen that are not immediately explainable, which is necessary, but the characters must not suspect it is just another reality warp. This requires a sense of the fixed everyday reality, which the regular micro movies provide. Finally, since the characters can't suspect Klingons, they are left with the hint of God, for what else could so contravened the laws of nature. Fixed everyday reality plus a cosmic intrusion: two seeming opposites, which is exactly the formula to allow the hint of God. If you allow too much flexibility in the reality they will always suspect Klingons or space time warps. If you allow no reality flexibility there will be nothing out of the ordinary. Consider a couple of examples of how this works.

In *Oh, God!* everyday reality is set in Burbank in the mundane life of an assistant manager of a Food World supermarket (John Denver). The intrusion: George Burns appearing/disappearing, making sounds, making it rain, etc. right in front of the assistant manager. Because this isn't science fiction, Jerry (Denver) doesn't suspect this appearance/disappearance thing is the work of the Klingons or a ripple in the space-time continuum. Throughout the movie it is always just another day in downtown Burbank. Nothing else is possible, which means that what Jerry has been witnessing can't be true, unless what this little old man is trying to tell him is true: he is, in fact, God. In *Field of Dreams* daily taken-for-granted reality takes the form of Iowa farm country, again, far, far away from R2D2 or C3PO. The rock of this middle American reality is Ray Kinsella (Kevin Costner), a simple, straight-shooting, ordinary, non-suspecting family man and corn farmer. The unexplained intrusion: that Voice speaking to him, "If you build it, he will come." Ray doesn't suspect Klingons either, nor his mental health. Daily Iowa reality holds tight; the Voice remains a mystery and is not naturalized. It is from the other side. That is the only possible explanation allowed by the setting of this film.

Or, consider a slight variation on this theme. Instead of metaphors of God and heaven, there is *Ground Hog Day,* a metaphor for hell. The ordinary reality here: February 2, Ground hog Day on a blustery cold winter day in Pennsylvania and a local news crew sent out to see if Puxutawney Phil, the ground hog, comes out to see his shadow. The cosmic intrusion: Phil, the obnoxious selfish weatherman played by Bill Murray, discovers that for him February 2 repeats, and repeats, and repeats. He goes to bed every night but when he wakes up it is February 2 again and again. He is trapped in time, in his own sort of hell. Now, instead of Phil the weatherman substitute Captain Piccard from *Star Trek*, or Luke Skywalker from *Star Wars*. If they were to awake and find it was the same day repeating, they would immediately suspect, ok, not the Klingons, I have used them too much already, but they would suspect someone, somehow, had managed to figure out some way to stop time, at least in this town on this day. The rest of the movie: figure out how to break their hold and free himself from the time machine. But Phil the weatherman has no such suspicions for his Pennsylvania reality allows no such speculation. Phil the weatherman, like Jerry the Food World assistant manager, and Ray the corn farmer is frustrated, confused and angry, at a reality that isn't obeying its own rules. He tries everything to get out of his own little hell, and finally does, but not by outfoxing the aliens or deciphering the time machinery.

A.J.B.

Notes

1. Mailer, Norman. 1998. "A Man Half Full." *New York Review of Books* (XLV, No. 20: 18).
2. Pym, John (ed.). 1998. *Time Out Film Guide.* 7th edition. London: Penguin Books.

14

Magical Realism and the Problem of Evil

> *"There are more things in heaven and earth,
> Horatio, than are dreamt of in your philoso-
> phy."*—Hamlet

Religion offers solutions to various critical situations recurring in individual lives. Through manifold forms and functions of ritual behavior and cultural interpretations, religion can still be seen to inhabit the deep vales of the landscape of life. Religion is in the tracks of biology, even if it is closely related to aboriginal invention of language, which brought the great opportunity for a shared mental world. At this level, what matters is not the success of the "selfish genes" in procreation, but coherence, stability and control within this world. This is what the individual is groping for, gladly accepting the existence of nonobvious entities or even principles. Baffling details of experience fall into place, and reality itself can have speech...

Insofar as the biological basis of life can hardly be abolished, "real" reality will make itself felt time and again...Humans will still not readily accept that constructs of sense reaching out for the nonobvious are nothing but self projections, and that no other signs from the universe around are there to be perceived except the irregularities resounding from the first big bang (Walter Burkert, *Creations of the Sacred: Tracks of Biology in Early Religions*, pp. 177-79).

Thus in his Gifford Lectures does Burkert challenge the project of those who for centuries have predicted the retreat of the influence of religion in the face of the steady and inexorable advance of science. His is an argument which would have been dismissed even a quarter century ago. Now as scholars discover the remarkable persistence of religion, there is perhaps less likelihood Burkert's position can be casually ignored. Sociologists like Rodney Stark and Philip Gorski have made powerful arguments against the triumph of "secularization" in the last several centuries. Lawrence Iannacone has demonstrated that religious devotion has not changed in European countries over the last hundred years. Ideology may be dead but religion lives.

But what about the "problem of evil" ask those who are skeptical? How do you explain why the "nonobvious" realities of Professor Burkert permit bad things to happen to good people. It is not our task in this book to answer that question. Rather we must show how the movies purport to answer it. If one is to agree with Burkert, how do films cope and present a response grounded in the hope that is biologically driven? Or perhaps more specifically how do the movies account for the joys and sorrows of life?

In this chapter I propose to consider the way that four films which I have grouped together under the rubric of "magical realism" purport to deal with death, especially the deaths of the young and the innocent.

The term is often applied to the work of South American novelists, Jorge Amado for example in his *Dona Flor and Her Two Husbands* and Gabriel Garcia Marquez in *Love in the Time of Cholera* and *One Hundred Years of Solitude*. In many of the works of these two great writers, the strange, the uncanny, the marvelous lurk at the edges. The reader can never be sure when the magical is suddenly going to appear and redirect the story. To the sober American Calvinist sensibility (which still dominates our society) there is a touch of the creepy in these incursions of the "supernatural." The Latino sensibility—like the Celtic—seems to take for granted that the strange and wonderful are ordinary components of human life. (42 percent of Americans report some kind of "real" contact with the dead.)

Do the practitioners of magical realism in fiction "really believe" in the magical? Such a question imposes the American agnostic perspective on men who don't find it pertinent. The world is magical, life is magical, what more needs to be said? Did Amado know of a woman whose marriage to a new husband seemed to be haunted by the spirit of her dead first husband? Doubtless he did. I do too for that matter. What a wonderful idea for a story! Did he *really* believe in "ghosts?" As someone who knew Amado personally, I'm sure he felt no need to answer that question. If pushed, his response might have varied with time and place and audience. He was, after all, a "pure materialist" as well as an "obo" in the voodoo cult—and when I baptized his grandson, he made the signs of the cross at all the appointed places and responded to the prayers with hearty "amens."

Marquez wrote that the reason some people found it hard to understand the marvelous in his fiction is that they think the dead are far away from us. In fact, he said, they are very close to us, a sensibility that the Celts share. Do I "really" believe that? Do I really agree with my Celtic ancestors (pagan and Christian) that the boundaries between the Land of Promise in the West and the world of daily life are thin and permeable, especially at times when one season edges into another? Do I really think that the "supernatural" lurks all around us? Do I really believe that the "magical" can be "realistic?"

The marvelous is at most a sign, not a proof, not an argument (and I can hear Amado laughing at that comment).

Sure, to all questions. I would not pretend to explain the metaphysics of the marvelous. I am one of the least "sensitive" of people. Yet I do believe that creation is "marvelous" and that in some fashion those who have gone before us are still with us. Moreover, I know many people, not at all superstitious or credulous, who have had brushes with the magical in the course of their realistic lives. So I think that the magical realists have an important insight into the human condition. The world is an open system, despite the Darwinists.

On the other hand, I don't believe that religious faith can or should be based on a constant search for ever more wonderful coincidences or miracles and I'm normally ready to dismiss (in my head if not in my words) claims about marvelous experiences. The magical realists have a point, but their point is not an adequate philosophy to say nothing of an adequate theology. The marvelous does happen occasionally (or perhaps more often than I think it does) but we cannot control it or use it or live by it.

Especially we cannot constrain it. "Magic" in the vocabulary of sociologists and anthropologists, refers to behavior (frequently ritual) in which people try to constrain the transcendent to respond on demand. If we perform this rite before we venture out to sea, then there will be no storms. If I pin this medal in my car, there will be no accidents no matter how I drive. "Magic" in this sense implies a contract with the transcendent: we do something and the transcendent has no choice but to do his part to live up to the contract. As will be clear in this chapter that is not the kind of magic about which I am writing. The transcendent in these four films acts entirely on his own initiative.

Would God ring nonexistent bells to validate the life of one of His holy ones? Maybe. Has She? I wouldn't put it past Him. She has done some pretty strange things.

So the magical realist films I propose to discuss are at best hints. There's nothing wrong with hints.

"Magical realism" is a term used especially of films of Spanish or Mexican origin. Perhaps *Like Water for Chocolate* is the best-known example of the genre. It is realistic because it deals with the ordinary conflicts and problems of life. Yet it is also magical because there are marvelous interventions which shape the course of the story. It is essential for the genre that the interventions be taken completely for granted by the characters. Yes, there is something miraculous which has happened, but, no, it is not surprising. Do not marvels happen every day?

I'm extending the genre to include films to which, as far as I know, no one has ever attributed the label. However, they deserve the title because they are utterly, indeed painfully realistic. Yet magical things happen, marvels which someone unseen seems to have deliberately introduced into the lives of the characters, especially in response to evil and suffering. While the characters are delighted by this intervention, they do not see it as any different from the other events of the story. Amado certainly and Marquez probably would enjoy them.

Perhaps the magic in the magical realism of the four films I will discuss is similar to the *deus ex machina* of the Greek tragedies in which a god or goddess was introduced (by a hook) to resolve the plot and save the day. Each of them demonstrates the willingness of a filmmaker to invoke Walter Burkert's "non-obvious" to confirm that there is more in the cosmos than perturbations of the primal big bang. The four filmmakers call in God to conclude their stories on a note of hope, indeed powerful and overwhelming hope. That they can get away with it is less a function of the religious belief of the critical fraternity than of the religious insensitivity of that profession. All four films are boldly religious, but those who depend on reviewers to decide what films they should see would never know that—unless, as in three of the four cases, they read Roger Ebert's reviews.

Did the filmmakers believe that there is a "non-obvious" out there–one indeed with a sense of humor and of irony–or are they only playing to the tastes and needs of their audiences, as critics often suggest? The question is irrelevant. Who knows what their intent was? Who cares? Does it matter whether Shakespeare believed in witches?

Commandments

Commandments, a 1996 film written and directed by Daniel Taplitz, explicitly deals with God's responsibility for human suffering. I found that each time I watched the film I liked it more. Despite its breezy and even lighthearted pace, it is ingenious and even subtle. Unfortunately for the film, most viewers would recognize its subtlety only in retrospect, if then. Not many critics or film watchers are familiar with the Book of Job, hence they missed the point that Seth Warner (Aidan Quinn) is Job. Either you know in the first five minutes that it is a redo of the Book of Job, or you never catch on and the film doesn't make much sense. Most people didn't catch on. *Commandments* disappeared quickly from the theaters, its magical realism overlooked completely, though Taplitz virtually beats his audience over the head with a two by four of magic in its conclusion.

The film begins with a phone call from Rachel Luce (Courteney Cox, whose name my male students invariably utter when I mention the film) to her husband Harry (Anthony LaPaglia). Seth Warner, who was married to her late sister, is standing on a roof screaming at God. Harry should go get him out of trouble. Harry, who doesn't believe in God or much of anything else except his own success and pleasure, doesn't see why they should care about Seth who is patently a loser, but he trots off to the scene. Seth and his dog Sparky are on the roof in pouring rain. Seth demands an explanation from God: Why has he lost his pregnant wife? Why was his house hit by a tornado which missed every other house on the street?

We see both tragedies in flashback. If we don't realize then that we are watching a modern version of the Job story, then we will be in deep trouble for the rest of the film. God—or someone—responds to Seth with a lightning bolt that knocks him and Sparky off the roof. Both survive, though Sparky loses a leg. Later in the hospital room where he is recovering Seth demands of Harry, what kind of God is it that picks on a harmless dog.

There are more trials awaiting Seth. When he returns to work, Seth's boss comes into his office and tells him he's fired and for no particular reason except that he doesn't want a man prone to such problems near him. For Seth this is the final blow. He has lost his wife, his child, his home, and his job. God has broken the Covenant with him. He will break it back. Harry doesn't get it. Why mess around with God? Even if there is a God, which Harry doubts, it's not a good idea to mess with him.

Harry plays the part of the false friends of Job who come to torment him while he's sitting on the dung hill bemoaning his fate. By now the signs that this is a Job story are so clear that only those who haven't read the book of Job—or perhaps haven't even heard of it—can fail to see what the film is about. To emphasize that we are in the world of the Jewish Scriptures, Rachel Luce is wrestling with the legal problems of a couple who discover a million dollars in their bank account. Rachel's bank wants the money back. But Mr. and Mrs. Adam don't have the money. They have given it to the Save the Whales campaign—a gift which telegraphs the end of the story.

Moreover the ten commandments are part of the Covenant which God made with Moses on Mount Sinai. It's a one-sided treaty. God proclaims, without having been asked, that He is Israel's God and they are His people. He is, God asserts, a passionately loving God and He does not want his people whoring around with false Gods ("I am the Lord, *Your* God). The commandments are part of the treaty. If Israel wants to act like a people God has chosen, then Israel will keep the commandments. Seth knows this, even if like every other religious theme and metaphor in the story, the critics don't.

I don't see how Daniel Taplitz could have been more explicit about the religious dimensions of the film or what more he could have done to explain to the critics what he was about. Maybe he has learned his lesson: with a few exceptions, film critics are a religiously illiterate crowd.

But Seth is not a religious illiterate. Having been influenced by both his father's rabbi and his mother's Irish Catholic priest, he knows what covenants are all about. He has kept his end of the bargain, God has not. Therefore he will terminate the covenant by breaking all the ten commandments. He even makes up a list and checks off each commandment as it is violated.

He goes to what looks like a Hindu religious service and worships there. He carves an idol and worships it. He dishonors the Sabbath. When his father persuades him to go to synagogue, he picks a fight at the Friday night service with the rabbi and thus dishonors his father.

Either God can prevent human suffering, he argues, and does not do so and therefore is cruel. Or God cannot prevent it and therefore he is not God. There is an uproar in the synagogue. Seth's father is furious. Seth leaves content that he has broken yet another commandment.

Already, all right, God. So there, too.

Seth has been living in a yuppie loft with Harry and Rachel. He sleeps in the room where Harry stores his prized collection of rare guitars, instruments which Harry admires but never plays. Rachel is nice to him, though at first she does not go beyond sympathy for her sister's widower. Harry, a sleazy investigative reporter, is pursuing a corrupt Irish police captain (in the movies all corrupt police captains are Irish!) and on the side is engaging in an affair with the captain's ditsy and dangerous girlfriend, one Melissa Murphy (Pamila Gray). Rachel suspects that her husband is unfaithful. Seth follows him to the girlfriend's home and discovers what is going on. He devises an ingenious plan to violate several commandments at the same time. He steals Harry's guitars and plants them in Melissa's house. Then he tips off the cops that Harry and Melissa have stolen the guitars and stashed them at her house so Harry can collect the insurance money. He already has coveted his neighbor's wife. All that remains is to make adulterous love to her and he will have broken the commandments against lying, stealing, coveting, and adultery. However, now he's in love with Rachel and can tell her honestly that he is not making love just to break another commandment.

He sees the eye of a hurricane on television, a hurricane that is expected to hit Long Island at Montauk, where his wife had died. In the eye of the storm he sees the Eye of God. He must go out to Montauk to hurl his last and final defiance at God: he will kill himself. Meanwhile Harry is released from jail and returns to his home to encounter both his wife and Melissa Murphy and Mr. and Mrs. Adam waiting out the hurricane. Rachel tells him she's pregnant and that Seth is the father. Seth has cost Harry his wife and his job. His brother-in-law, he decides, is a crazy man. The only commandment he has not violated is "thou shalt not kill." Harry must kill him before Seth kills Harry to complete his vendetta against God.

(There's no explanation, by the way, of how Rachel is aware a day or two after her romp with Seth that she is carrying his child.)

They meet in a surrealistic scene on the Montauk lighthouse as the rains and the wind batter the building and the storm, presumably the Eye of God, howls around them. Neither can kill each other. Seth finishes his campaign against God by throwing himself into the seething ocean. Now he has violated all the commandments.

Until this scene the film has been all realism, a quirky story in which God is present only as a target for Seth's rage. The story of Job has been told in modern guise. The modern Job does not say, "Blessed is the name of the Lord." Rather he kills himself to punish God. The next morning, however, the magic starts.

The storm is gone. The sky is blue, the water is calm, the rubble liters the beach at Montauk. A crowd of people stroll along the beach and come upon the body of a dead whale. One of the men slits the whale's belly (Why? Don't ask, this is a movie after all!). Water pours out and then fish the whale has swallowed. Suddenly a man's foot protrudes from the whale's belly. Some of the people pull the rest of him out. Who is it? Jonah? No, it's Job—Seth Warner whom God has thrown back from the waves! The story of Job ends with the sign of Jonah!

This is pretty dramatic stuff. God trumps Seth Warner's rage with love. None of Seth's questions are answered, but, like Job, he has a new wife (who joins him on the beach) a new child, and a new life. He now knows better than to ask the questions that so tormented him. God's love always triumphs. It does no good to fight God because God won't fight back.

The film ends with Harry sitting on a roof. Sparky is with him. Seth gets the woman, Harry gets the dog. It's all right he tells us that's just the way things work out. Is there a God? Harry doubts it. You just make life more difficult than it is, if you add that problem to your life. Still there might be. So Harry stands up and shouts defiance at God, just in case, as the credits come up.

Taplitz, who clearly knows his Bible pretty well, must have chortled often to himself that he was able to change the ending to the Job story by adding on the Jonah story. It is a memorable tour de force even if most people didn't get it. There is no answer, he tells us, to the problem of evil and suffering, no more today than there was in the time of Job. The only response available to humans is the response that was available to Job. One must yield one's trust entirely to one's faith that God loves us as dearly beloved children even when, a la Seth Warner, we act like idiots.

Jonah's whale on the beach at Montauk is magic realism with a vengeance. Everything else on the beach the day after the storm is perfectly normal, ordinary, commonplace. Yet a man comes out of the belly of a dead whale.

And with that resurrection life begins again.

Truly, Madly, Deeply

The realism of *Truly, Madly, Deeply*, an English film (1991) written and directed by the Anglo-Italian filmmaker Anthony Minghella, is more gentle and the magic more subtle than both characteristics are in *Commandments*. Early on we are persuaded that it is perfectly ordinary and routine that Nina (Juliet Stevenson) encounters her dead lover, a cellist named Jamie (Alan Rickman), in the rickety apartment they once shared. Don't lovers always or at least often come back from the dead?

(In fact, many perfectly reasonable and sensible people will claim to have had such experiences, but that issue is beyond the scope of this analysis.)

The most magical part of this magical (in many different ways) story is the message the dead lover (and his friends) convey to Nina. Equally magical is the image of God, a lacy white cloud drifting across the sky. At one point in the film, Jamie looks out of the window of the apartment, glances up at the sky and sees the cloud. He suddenly becomes very serious and respectful. The cloud doesn't frighten him. Rather it warns him that he is on very serious business which he must bring to a conclusion.

Jamie and Nina had been deeply in love. He dies, suddenly and senselessly, from a "cold." Nina is devastated with grief. Her colleagues at work (she teaches English to immigrants from Spanish-speaking countries), her students, her friends, the men who are constantly at work repairing her apartment, all try to cheer her up. Some of the men hint delicately at the possibility of a new relationship (with them). One of them, a Polish immigrant, is much more direct and forthright. Nina is trapped in her grief. She does not want to escape. Somehow it would betray Jamie if she permitted life to go on. She tells her therapist how she imagines Jamie with her, talking to her as she walks down the streets of London. She asks the therapist if that is strange. The therapist replies with the standard question of whether Nina thinks it strange.

Incidentally, Minghella's cinematography of London makes it look like Tuscany. In his world apparently cloudy and rainy days are rare in that city, a form of magic in itself.

Her sister, an awkward and insensitive woman, even asks her whether they might buy Jamie's cello so that her son can use it in his cello lessons. Nina is deeply offended that Jamie's belongings are considered appropriate for second-hand purchase. The sister retreats clumsily.

Then one night she comes home to her crumbling apartment, notices that some of the furniture has been moved back to the way it was when Jamie lived in it, and then hears his cello. It's not a ghost, not really. Rather it's Jamie, just the way he was when he was alive. He's dead of course and he speaks vaguely about the hereafter. He's also very cold. He has to dress in warm clothes and keep the temperature in the apartment high. But it's Jamie all right, gentle, prickly, witty, and politically radical. They spar with one another frequently, just as they did when he was "alive."

Minghella discretely draws the curtain on the intimacy of their relationship. Do they make love? Probably, but we don't see it and it's never mentioned. Is it really Jamie come back from the dead to console his grieving beloved or is it a trick of Nina's imagination? Or somehow both? One hint that it's not just her imagination, but something truly magical is that the rats which had plagued her apartment suddenly disappear.

Her friends and colleagues notice her happiness and wonder what has caused it. She realizes that she cannot tell them that Jamie is back from the dead. She must hide him and keep everyone else out of the apartment.

Then she is having a coffee with one of her students (a beautiful young woman, unmarried but in the advanced stages of pregnancy) in a coffee shop. An argument explodes between the owner of the shop and the waiter who, like the pregnant woman, is a political refugee. The owner accuses the waiter of stealing from him. The waiter replies proudly that he never steals and that he is an honorable man, indeed a physician in his home country. A young man who is drinking coffee by himself eases the tension with several magic tricks.

Nina finds the young man attractive. His name is Mark and he works with severely "challenged" young people. The white cloud floats across the sky as their relationship develops. Mark (Michael Maloney) is, as Roger Ebert observes, goofy and charming. He represents the invitation of life. But Nina cannot give up her dead and yet somehow still living lover for Mark, even though Mark has obviously fallen in love with her.

Then the magic increases. Several of Jamie's musical colleagues from the hereafter show up in her house to watch videos and play Mozart quartets. Nina is offended. They are making a mess of her apartment. "I can't believe I have a bunch of dead people watching videos in my living room!" She's even more upset when they roll back a carpet because the floor provides better resonance for their music.

The student delivers her baby. Nina goes to the hospital (or to hospital as the Brits would say) and holds the child in her arms. Life offers yet another appeal. Mark wants to see her again. She goes back to the apartment and has it out with Jamie. He seems to understand. She leaves. The other dead men gather around Jamie. Is this it? they ask. He frowns ponders and agrees that yes, this is it. They seem happy.

They rush to the window to watch Nina walking down the street for her date with Mark. They grin and raise their thumbs up. Their work has been successful. Jamie has come back not to reclaim his love but to free her. The next day the rats are back in the apartment. She packs the cello for her nephew. Life goes on.

The fabric of *Truly, Madly, Deeply* is delicate and fragile, like a carefully created lace coverlet. *Commandments* beats you over the head with its response to the problem of evil. *Truly, Madly, Deeply* deals with evil in a far more subtle, almost flimsy way. Of all the movies in which God appears, none depict a less pushy God or, one might say, a more ingenious God. An attractive young man and the birth of a baby gently charm Nina away from her grief. Did she really need the disturbing presence of her dead lover and his colleagues to persuade her that the only possible response to evil in life is to go on with life? Perhaps, perhaps not. Might it be that the prospect of living, human love is the only answer to the problem of evil? Might it be that grief must be put aside—not denied, not forgotten, not repressed— so that one can continue to respond to the prospects of life? Must one finally let go of grief and anger, though not of memory? Is the only way to win a victory over death defiance? When the Irish made love in the fields (up to the middle of the last century) they were saying in effect, "screw you, death!" Finally is that kind of defiance necessary to provide some closure to grief?

Grief and rage (towards whomever or whatever caused or seemed to cause the loss of love) is precious. Humans cling to it desperately. It is easy to say trippingly on the tongue that grief and rage must eventually be surmounted. One who tries to console is wise to keep his mouth shut until the grieving person begins to see the need to transcend (not forget) grief.

Jamie and his friends have come back to edge Nina, perhaps none too gently, in the direction of transcendence, to push her in the direction that Mark and the new baby invite her. Jamie can get away with such pushing because he is, after all, the lover for whom she is mourning. One cannot imagine a lost lover wanting anything but such transcendence. A mourner does not in fact honor the lost love by fixating on that person. But no one can tell a person that until in fact the person begins to see for himself. There are many different ways of dealing with grief, none better than others. But they all come to the same when a person is ready to go on: choose for life instead of for death.

Minghella's magical realism responds to the problem of evil with the very modest assertion life is at least as strong as death and maybe stronger. One does not need a dead whale on a beach to believe that life endures.

And the lacy white cloud continues to drift benignly across the sky, inviting us to more abundant life.

Household Saints

Are saints crazy? Can crazy people become saints? Can one tell the difference between a crazy person and a saint? Such questions haunt much recent Catholic art and literature. Saints are, it would seem, single-minded persons. They are not like anyone else. A recent book, by a Jesuit psychiatrist, on St. Ignatius of Loyola asks whether the founder of the Jesuits was a neurotic and concludes that he was. It also asks whether he was a saint and concludes that he was. Finally it asks whether the neuroticism actually facilitated his growth in sanctity and concludes that it did. It is unlikely that Nancy Savoca, the brilliant Italian-American filmmaker who directed and wrote (along with producer Richard Guay) *Household Saints*, has read the book but her conclusion is the same. Teresa Carmela Santangelo (and all three names are important) may be just a little bit neurotic—or if you wish—a whole lot neurotic. She may even have suffered a severe psychotic interlude. Yet still....Well, the Italian-American women who talk about her several years after death at the beginning of the film have no doubt about it: Teresa Carmela Santangelo was and is a saint.

The problem of evil in *Household Saints* is illustrated by the early death of a lovely and generous young woman who might have had a long and happy life if were not, as a very modern and up-to-date nun-psychiatrist tells her parents, for the fact that she had religious delusions and pietistic obsessions. Did religion drive her insane? Or did it make her a saint? Or was there some strange combination of the two at work in her life?

In passing and with all do respect to Martin Scorsese and his genius for making films about Italian-American community life, Nancy Savoca has an even better feel for the settings and scenes of that life from the 1950s until the present and the continuity and the change in those scenes. If a couple of centuries in the future, Italian-American historians wonder what Italian life was like at the tail end of the twentieth century, they would do well to consider Ms. Savoca's films.[1]

To begin the Italian-American matron who is telling the story says, her father won her mother in a pinochle game. You could tell that she was going to be a saint. Joseph Santangelo (Vincent D'Onofrio), sausage maker, is in love with Catherine Falconetti (Tracy Ullman), the daughter of his neighbor across the street who is also part of a neighborhood pinochle club. Catherine, a somewhat slatternly and outspoken woman wants no part of him. But in a high-stakes game, Joseph wins the right to marry Catherine. Joseph's mother doesn't think much of Catherine and is especially contemptuous of her cooking. Catherine on the other hand sees something more in Joseph than she had perceived in him before. Despite Mrs. Santangelo's skepticism, the young couple marry. They spend the wedding night in the Santangelo apartment with the mother in the next bedroom. Nonetheless, they enjoy one another ("O Santangelo!" Catherine shouts at the time of her fulfillment, "O Holy Angel!") and begin a marriage that is always happy.

The mother is a constant problem. Her religion is a mixture of Catholic piety and superstition, with a heavy dose of the latter. The walls are somber and covered with holy pictures. But there is magic in the house already. She has long conversations with Joseph's father who has been dead for many years. She sees him and so do we. Her constant harassment of Catherine drives the young woman into a miscarriage of their first child, which appears to the distraught young woman to be a dead chicken just as Mrs. Santangelo had foretold.

There is a flash of light one day in the apartment, Joseph's father appears, and the old woman goes off with him. The holy pictures come down, the apartment is repainted, and a daughter—Teresa Carmela is born, named after St. Teresa the Carmelite mystic. The little girl grows up intensely religious, more like her paternal grandmother than either of her parents. The Catholic school scenes set in the late 1950s and early 1960s are remarkably accurate and poignant. From the beginning Teresa wants to be a nun. She reads avidly the autobiography of St. Thérèse of Lisieux, the so-called Little Flower. (Sister Thérèse of the Infant Jesus and the Holy Face, as she was called in her day in the Carmelite convent—where she died at the age of twenty-four).

I'm a great admirer of Thérèse (now deservedly a Doctor of the Church) and especially of her robust common sense, her love of the beautiful, and her ability to laugh at herself. It seemed to me, as I watched the teenage Teresa Carmela (Lili Taylor), that she lacked all three of these saving characteristics and that she strove to imitate her patron with an almost fundamentalist literalism that was unhealthy.

But what do I know?

Her parents, now well dressed and well groomed and clearly successful, do not want her to be a nun. "My daughter isn't going to sacrifice her life, just to put money in the Pope's pocket," Joseph shouts. With the pious and unsmiling docility—innocent of affect—that marks all her behavior, Teresa accepts their decision as God's will. She leaves everything in God's hands. She wants only to be his servant and do all things well for God, even and especially the little things (as her patron had preached).

I confess that Teresa Carmela gave me the creeps. I had known young women like her when I was in parish work. They had gone off to convents, came home from them, and entered marriages which were frightfully unhappy. In both the religious life and in marriage, they had made choices for self-sacrificial reasons that were unwise and unhealthy.

If Teresa Carmela is a saint, then maybe they are too. But what do I know!

An ambitious yuppie, one Leonard Villanova, seduces Teresa and she moves in with him. Her parents, bitterly opposed to the convent, seem less opposed to her being a doormat for Lenny than for the Pope. Teresa accepts it all as God's will. Since she was unable to become a nun, she tells herself, God sent Leonard for her to love and take care of. One day when she is ironing Len's red and white checked shirt, Jesus appears in the small flat she and Len share, and talks to her. Then the flat is filled with hundreds of red and white shirts. Her parents come and Teresa is removed to an asylum.

She is serenely content there, as though it were the convent she wanted to join. On a cold and snowy spring day her parents travel on the train out into the countryside to see her. She is in bed, ill from an undiagnosed disease, but incredibly beautiful and ecstatically happy. She tells her parents that she has been playing pinochle with St. Thérèse, God the Father, and Jesus. She and St. Thérèse always lose, because the saint is not very good and because God the Father cheats. This surprises her, she says, because God doesn't have to cheat because he's going to win anyway. However, she doesn't seem to mind this oddity.

Late that night the parents receive a call. Teresa Carmela has died in her sleep, cause undetermined. The next morning they return to find her in the same bed, hands folded, eyes closed, a crucifix in her hand, looking as alive as she had seemed the day before. Joseph claims that there is a scent of roses in the room. Catherine denies it. On the way back to the city, Joseph says that the garden in front of the home, in glorious full bloom as they leave, was barren the day before. Catherine insists that it had been blooming the day before.

I had to rewind the tape. Joseph was right. On the day of their visit the garden was a mess of dead stems and sludge. Magical realism, always lurking in the film, has now exploded.

At her wake Teresa Carmela is already hailed as a saint.

No matter what anyone thought about her obsessions and delusions, God had validated his beloved as a saint.

I still think she was kind of creepy. But, like I say, what do I know.

To risk exegesis on the story is to violate it. Perhaps Ms. Savoca is saying that although Teresa Carmela did not understand her patron and although there was much that was compulsive about her struggle for sanctity, God accepted her efforts for the generosity that marked them and not for their wisdom or prudence. Perhaps God was saying, hey, I make my saints wherever I want to make them, despite nun-psychiatrists and priest sociologists.

Who can argue with that?

Did she really talk to Jesus? The answer has to be, "Who knows!" She was a good and generous and loving young woman who, apparently died of love at the age of twenty-four, just as did her patron.

Household Saints sweeps away the problem of evil with a rich Italianate wave of the hand: God takes care of all of his beloved children, of which Teresa Carmela Santangelo is only one of the more responsive.

Or as Roger Ebert said as he ended his review, "when did it become madness to want to be a saint?"

Breaking the Waves

The realism component of magical realism in *Breaking the Waves* (1996) is harsh, much more so than the realism in the previous three films. Lars von Trier has created a world of physical, moral, and emotional harshness. The magic which appears at the end, the most dramatic in any movie I have ever seen, contrasts vividly with the harshness and indeed overwhelms it and redeems the film. One hundred and fifty-eight minutes of agony are transformed in less than a minute. I suspect many of us who sat through those first 157 minutes were tempted to walk out. At the conclusion of the film we were glad that we did not —though its length is perhaps self-indulgent.

(I work on the premise that if a filmmaker cannot do what he wants to do in less than two hours, indeed less than an hour and a half, then he will not be able to do it in two and a half or three hours. But then what do I know?)

Von Trier is a Catholic Dane. He may well exhaust the population of Danish Catholic filmmakers. *Breaking the Waves* is a classic exercise in the Catholic imagination, an imagination which sees the sacred lurking everywhere, as well as an almost perfect example of magical realism in film as a means for dealing with the problem of evil. Taplitz is Jewish. Presumably Minghella and Savoca have at least a Catholic background (Ms. Savoca almost had to have attended Catholic schools). Is there something in the Catholic and (Orthodox?) Jewish worldviews that inclines artists with such a religious perspective to see magic all around? Certainly literary magical realism flourishes especially in Central and South American contexts.

Vastly different from *Household Saints*, *Breaking the Waves* has the same response to the problem of evil—God vindicates his beloved children, especially when they are saints. Or as Roger Ebert put it in his review, "God not only knows everything, he understands far more than we give him credit for."

The setting is a barren island off the coast of Scotland with oil rigs just over the horizon. The protagonist is Bess (Emily Watson), a simple young woman who is in love with an oil worker named Jan (Stellan Skarsgard). The bearded elders of her rigidly fundamentalist congregation (of which her grandfather is one of the leaders) disapprove of the wedding, but yield to her insistence.

In the disk version of the film we learn that Bess cannot read because of a learning disability. She spends much of her time in the church dusting and cleaning. She speaks to God as a naïve and innocent child. She imagines that God responds to her in her own voice which, when God is speaking, sounds like that of a gruff but patient and sympathetic adult. The religious temper of the congregation is revealed by the fact that the elders have taken the bells out of the bell tower and that they consign people they judge to be sinners to graves at the edge of a cliff overlooking the ocean with the verdict that the deceaseded will be in hell for all eternity. Women may not speak in church, nor attend burial services.

They seem to enjoy such rituals.

Von Trier is furious at such self-righteous hypocrisy. At first I thought that he was taking cheap shots at sitting ducks. It is easy to make sport of the radical fundamentalists. Then it dawned on me that similar phoniness can be found in every denomination, including my own.

Bess may not be very bright, but she is capable of great love and eager to be loved. She drags her new husband off to the powder room during their wedding party and tells him he can love her now. Then she asks what she is supposed to do. Marital sex for her is transformative just as it was for Catherine in *Household Saints*. Bess is ecstatically happy. In church she thanks God for having sent Jan to love her. God seems pleased that she likes his gift.

However, when Jan must go back to the rig, Bess falls apart. She is moody, melancholy, profoundly unhappy. She complains to God who replies that she should be satisfied. She begs him to send Jan back from the rig. Jan indeed comes back from the rig paralyzed from an accident. You wanted him back, didn't you? God replies unsympathetically.

Unable to move, staying alive on tubes, Jan worries about what will happen to Bess without sexual love. He urges her to find another man. Naturally she refuses. Then he begs her to make love to men and tell him about it, so he can enjoy her accounts.

There is considerable debate about this apparently cruel behavior of Jan. Has his knowledge of how important sexual love is to Bess become twisted or in his sickness is he too confused to know what he's doing—does he simply want Bess to get used to living without him? Von Trier chooses to leave us uncertain about many things in the story.

Bess talks it over with God. What can she do to cure poor Jan? God tells her that Jan has already described what she must do. Bess cannot believe God is telling her to commit adultery. Yet if that's what she must do, then she will do it.

Does God actually tell her this or are all her conversations with God imaginary? Did Teresa Carmela really see Jesus?

Bess obediently throws herself at the doctor who is taking care of Jan. He declines. She tries to fake an account to Jan. He sees through her pretense and demands that she do the real thing. So Bess becomes a prostitute, serving the ships anchored off shore. She dresses like a tart, but manages to look only like an innocent pretending to be tart. She is thrown out of the church and stoned by the children of the congregation. Finally she decides she must go to a ship in the bay which other prostitutes shun because of the violent men on it. She asks God whether he will be with her wherever she goes. Now God, no longer like her fundamentalist cleric but gentle and loving, assures her that he will always be with her.

She goes out to the ship in the darkness. In darkness she also returns, beaten, wounded, almost dead. She dies in the hospital with Jan, now able to limp to her side, looking on. She has sacrificed her life for her husband.

Or has she? What does it all mean? Did God really expect her to play the whore? Or did she misunderstand what God wanted? Who knows? Those questions are not to the point. The point rather is that her love, however misguided, was total and complete. Did she have to die that Jan might recover? Did she pay a price for his salvation? As one of my nephews remarked, "once you know she's a Christ figure, everything else fits into place."

Or, more generally, don't try to parse metaphors.

The elders decide that she may be buried but there will be no church services for her. Rather she will be buried at the side of the ocean. But as the casket is laid in the ground, we notice sand leaking from it. Bess's body is not in the tomb over which the elders pronounce their solemn malediction. Rather it is out on the oil rig where Jan, now almost completely cured, and his friends bury her with honor at sea. Jan hobbles back to his bunk. When morning comes, the radio man dashes into his compartment. You've got to hear this, he says. It's everywhere!

Mighty and joyous bells peal over the rig and over the ocean and over the land. The final image of the film is to bells pealing in the empty bell tower of the wee kirk. God has vindicated His servant! In the peal of the bells, the harshness and ugliness of the film is transformed into glorious triumph. Was it really God speaking to her? Did Jesus really visit Teresa Carmela? Irrelevant questions in the final analysis. Great love, even when misguided, says the magical realist, invites great love in return—despite all the stone-throwing, to-hell-damning hypocrites in the world.

A hundred and fifty-six minutes of harsh and ugly realism, one minute of magic and we all know what has happened. God has found another saint.

*   *   *

The God in the movies like *All That Jazz* and *Always* is a pragmatically passionate God, one who pursues us with an implacable love, a God who begs us to let go of life so that we might find more life. The God of magical realism is a God of enormous power, a God who can make bells ring even when there are no bells, a God who causes a spring garden to bloom overnight despite the snow, a God who saves a drowning man in a body of a whale, a God who can send the dead back to free a survivor of paralyzing grief. If the tender passion of God's love is often missed in weekend homilies and sermons, the triumphant power of God's love is even more often overlooked. If God can take care of Seth, Nina, Teresa Carmela, and Bess, then She can and will take care of all the rest of Her beloved children.

So the filmmakers seem to be hinting. We too may be caught up in the Magical Realism game, we may be participants not spectators no matter what goes wrong with our lives.

Two questions arise immediately: Is God really like that? Do the filmmakers really think He is or are they just, as some of the critics suggest, merely pandering the religious faith of their audiences?

The second question is insulting, especially when addressed to the four filmmakers in this chapter. Moreover, it is irrelevant, save to critics who want to explain away the sensibility of these films. The images of God which permeate these movies may be wrong. There may be no God at all. God may exist but not care about us. Or God might be powerless to do anything to help us, as much as He would like to. There is substantial evidence to support such perspectives. Argue, if you want, that Taplitz, Minghella, Savoca, and von Trier are wrong. Do not argue that they are fakers.

The first question is the pertinent one. Is the God of Magical Realism real? Is She the kind of God who can and will take care of us as She takes care of Seth, Nina, Teresa Carmela, and Bess? Is She, finally, what Teresa's patron saint once said, "nothing but mercy and love?"

Powerful mercy and passionate love.

God may not be that at all, but then He's not God. No God worthy of the name would be anything else than what the magical realists imply. Either a power like that is at the core of the cosmos, or the universe is meaningless. Most humans as Walter Burkert observed will not easily accept such a conclusion.

Magical Realism as a genre and these magical films in particular suggest that the higher power whom they invoke to spit Seth out of the whale, to send Jamie back to free Nina, to vindicate Teresa and Bess is merely anticipating what eventually He will do for all of us.

This is a very attractive notion. It may be wrong, but it is nonetheless attractive. Moreover it is certainly not wrong simply because it is attractive.

The magical realism movies about God are deeply religious, usually explicitly so. They are also in debt to the visions of the western religious heritages. One continues to wonder why the films make these visions so much more appealing than the official guardians and practitioners of these heritages are currently able to make them. Indeed one wonders why so many of the officials of the heritages resemble Bess's tormentors rather than the God to whom she talks and who finally vindicates her.

A.M.G.

Note

1. I must confess that I saw *Household Saints* for the first time in 1994 and thought it charming. Though I had already been working on my *God in the Movies* project for some years then, I was blind to its relevance for that project. Only when I saw it on cable in the summer of 1998 did I realize that it fit perfectly into the project. Perhaps *Breaking the Waves* sensitized me to the fact that *Household Saints* was about God.

15

European Novel, American Movie, Japanimation: The Evolution of Storytelling

I would like to conclude with a preliminary discussion of where the types of movies we have been considering fit into the larger evolution of cultural formats used for narrative, or storytelling. To do this I want to go back a few hundred years and speculate a little about the future. From poems to novels to live theater, there have been any number of cultural forms used for storytelling prior to the advent of cinema in the twentieth century. As these change over the centuries, so, too, do the regions where they are developed and most often reach their technological and aesthetic potential. For instance, the past few hundred years were dominated by Europe both politically—economic might, colonial extension, and so forth—and culturally, as the European novel and theater were carried by colonialism and emulated around the globe. Into the twentieth century there was an observable shift in global economic prowess from Europe to the United States and not accidentally I think, a new form of cultural expression emerged, the movie, which, as the century progressed bypassed the novel as the central "literature" of the day. Non-Europeans have written novels, yet the leading exemplars were European; likewise others made movies, yet the leading examples came primarily from the country in which this new form of expression was developed, the United States. There seems to have been, then, a correlation between dominant geo-political zone and the innovation of cultural forms of expression.

This brings us to the twenty-first century. Can we make a reasonable guess about possible new forms of expression that might supercede the movies someday? I think so. Let's start with what we presently know. In the nineteenth- to twentieth-century transition from Europe to America we saw a shift in both the location of global political/economic strength and in the dominant form of cultural expression, from European play/ novel to American movies. If this is more than a spurious correlation then perhaps there is some causal association between global political and cultural dominance. One way to examine this hypothesis is to look for evidence of both the successor to North America in economic prowess and indicators of new forms of expression that might be twenty-first-century successors to the live action movie. Starting with shifts in economic hegemony, trends in global production and trade suggest that East Asia is the best guess to succeed North America as the most dynamic region of the world economy (Bergesen and Fernandez, 1999).

The evidence here, which is still a matter of extrapolating present trends, is nonetheless clearer than identifying a clear successor to the live action film. If, though, we extrapolate the cutting edge trend in moviemaking, digitalized computer generated (CG) imagery for special effects then it is possible to speculate that some time in the twenty-first century filmed, live action—the bedrock of movies for the past one hundred years—may very well give way to various forms of animated/computer generated feature-length movies. The continuation of this trend into hologramic projections has long been predicted, but we will only deal here with the potential for the shift to the virtual reality of CG animation. Given this trend, which let's tentatively assume will eventually displace filmed live action, where in the world will it be developed to its fullest as storytelling medium. That is, if the novel/ play was developed to its fullest in Europe, the movie in America, where will the geo-origination/development site be for animation?

One obvious possibility is the U.S., where computer generated special effects have been magnificently interwoven with live action. But this may not be the case, for there seems to be a necessary shift in the geo-economic foundation which undergirds the development of new forms of storytelling. Europe, for example, led in the development of the novel, but this advantage was not translated into a leading position with the novel's successor, cinema. That advantage went to the U.S. instead, which also succeeded Europe as the world's dominant economic region. Trends suggest East Asia will be the successor to North

America as the lead sector of the world economy, and if the process I am suggesting here is general, then East Asia should also be the lead area in developing CG/animation storytelling.

For evidence of this possibility, consider the direction of moviemaking in Japan, the most advanced East Asian economy. What is most striking here is the incredible popularity of animation for telling all sorts of stories: "In Japan animation seems ever more ready to overwhelm 'human' cinema entirely" (Server 1999: 88). For example, upon its release the 1997 animated feature *Mononoke Hime* (*The Princess Mononoke*) broke the fifteen-year earnings record for a first-run movie that had been held by *E.T. the Extra-Terrestrial* and became the then highest grossing film in Japanese history. Such Japanimation, or *"animie,"* is animation quite different from the simple children's stories of Disney-like American animation, as here it involves well-written stories, beautiful graphics, and often explicit violence and sexuality. This animation has its origins in *"manga,"* Japanese comic books, many of which have been made into movies and television programs. Manga comics are mainly in black and white, while the animated videos and movies are in color. Osamu Tezuka, who created the first animated TV series, *Tetuswan Atom* (Astro Boy, when released in the U.S.) was the first to use movie techniques like close-ups and long shots to achieve desired dramatic effects. His dramatic styling of large eyes and small nose, has been copied by others and is the hallmark of animie. In the 1970s and 1980s such animated stories became more popular when the animie *Robotech* was released. Perhaps the best known of the anime is *Akira (1988)*, although *Ghost in the Shell* (1995) is also well known, and *Princess Mononoke* (1997) which is set for worldwide distribution, may yet be the best known of the anime movies. Disney has contracted to distribute *Princess Mononoke* worldwide along with the other anime films of *Mononoke*'s director and creator Miyazaki Hayao. Disney believes such Japanese animated features are the future direction of animation and they want to be involved in co-production and worldwide distribution. While the look of Japanimation is strikingly innovative and unique, of more sociological importance is the fact that it is used for a much fuller range of narrative tasks than animation in the U.S. There are science fiction, romance, horror, historical, ninja/martial arts, comedy, soap opera/everyday life, true story, adults only, ultra-violence, war, adventure, and suitable-for-kids categories of anime (McCarthy, 1997: 11).

The Princess Mononoke, for instance, is not a traditional children's animation in the vein of American musical cartoons. It has a very complex and adult script: "Set in a demon-haunted world during Japan's feudal era...[it] tells in terms of allegorical fantasy of the battle between humankind, on the verge of becoming industrialized, and the creatures and gods of nature, who are being supplanted in the process. The title character is a feral young woman who, after being abandoned in infancy, is raised by giant wolves and becomes their leader in battle against the humans. It is not 'Pocahontas'" (Mallory, 1998). For a contrast, compare this to Disney's website description of their animated feature *Toy Story 2:* "The fun and adventure continue when Andy goes off to summer camp and the toys are left to their own devices. Things shift into high gear when an obsessive toy collector kidnaps Woody....It's now up to Buzz Lightyear and the gang from Andy's room—Mr. Potato Head, Slinky Dog, Rex, and Hamm—to spring into action and save their pal from winding up a museum piece." It's not that children's animations aren't made in Japan; they are, and their descriptions would no doubt sound similar. The point, though, is that most American animation releases are only such light children's fantasy. While *Pocahontas, Mulan* or *The Prince of Egypt* are a little more "serious" they are still primarily youth fare.

This wider breadth of animated storytelling genres suggests that when the technology of CG imagery develops even then it will be countries such as Japan that possess the cultural inclination, or ability, to utilize that technology to the fullest. The Americans, while having pioneered animation techniques, seem trapped in children's programs. It appears that Japan is as comfortable and innovative with animation as the U.S. was with film and as Europe was even earlier with the novel/play. What this suggests is that the technological edge attained by the world economy's leading area can be translated into new technologies of storytelling. In the case of animation, developments like digital camera technology, as perfected by the Japanese firm Sony, will allow moviemakers to avoid film completely and in combination with computer generated imagery be able to realize any scene that can be imagined. The 100-year reign of chemically developed film is coming to an end. As today's CD and DVD disk players transform digital information into sound and images, the same will occur with digitally encoded principal photography which can be downloaded from satellites, completely altering the way movies are made and distributed.

The U.S., with its comparative advantage in film, will certainly benefit from such developments, as digital technology can be used to project traditional 35-millimeter film by making a digitalized print, thus cutting costs. It can also be used along with computer generated imagery to increase the special-effects component of the traditional live action movie. But even with such advances storytelling will still be done within the traditional live action format whose reality creates limits on the visual images that can be constructed. That is, filming live people, places, and objects brings their fixed natural boundaries, colors, sizes, voices, and range of motion into the moviemaking process, which limits the pure imaginative freedom of moviemakers. The people and things of live action can be manipulated, staged, put in front of a CG background, and even interact with CG characters, but their given reality has to be adapted to by the moviemaker, such that ultimate possibilities offered by growing digitalization and CG imagery will have a natural limit for a moviemaking process whose principal photography is based on filming live action.

Animation, on the other hand, has no such restraints imposed by the substance of things being filmed, because there aren't any. If it can be imagined it can appear on screen, and the growing digitalized technology of computer generated imagery that is advancing in the twenty-first century will be of more benefit to a storytelling imagination based on animation rather than filmed live action. While the medium for representation gets more and more simulated, it can, ironically, represent more and more reality. Less and less of the real represents more and more reality. An interesting development. For instance, how much of Renaissance England can be realistically represented on an Elizabethan stage? Parts of a few buildings, a room, not much. If the play is about Julius Caesar, how much of ancient Rome? In movies, though, with elaborate historical sets, *Ben Hur, The King of Kings,* and *Cleopatra* could represent a much more realistic sense of ancient Rome. What about pre-historic times when dinosaurs roamed the earth. How realistically is that represented on the stage? Even in the movie *Godzilla* it was just a man in a rubber suit, sloshing along in a pond of water simulating a T-Rex-like creature walking out of Tokyo Bay. But the sense of realism was far exceeded in the computer-generated dinosaurs in *Jurassic Park*. Here was pure animation/computer generated imagery, the most virtual medium, yet the most realistic representation of all. Interesting.

American filmmakers will adapt but they will not be able to transcend their earlier advantage in filmed live action, such that they will, in the twenty-first century, produce something of a hybrid form of movie: part filmed live action and part CG animation. It's the best of American moviemaking today, and form-wise, it is, I think, about as far toward a purely animated format the American moviemaking imagination will go. CG will increase, as special effects and for more principal photography, but the American movie, as we know it, will not evolve into the animation features we now see developing in Japan. This will result in some great art, but in terms of the continuing evolution of storytelling, the center of new forms of expression will shift to a new geo-economic region, Asia.

This same process has been repeated before. Europe enjoyed the comparative advantage prior to the twentieth century in novel and play format. Then came the rise of cinema. The leading edge shifted to the U.S., which maximized the narrative potentials of the movies the same way the Japanese are now pressing animation into full narrative service. The Europeans would go on to make movies in the twentieth century, but they would no longer be the dominant center; that shifted to the U.S. What they did is what the Americans will do with the shift to animation. They go part way. They make movies, but they are, by and large, small personal stories told in a very realistic vein, that could be described as part novel/play and part pure cinema. Europeans simply don't make blockbusters, epics, special-effects ridden science fiction, horror, children's animated cartoons (Disney), or any of the other movie genres in which the Americans are so active. Their cultural investment in the realism and intimate scale of the novel holds European filmmakers to personal, small-scale, very dramatic stories. European movies were always more "filmed plays" than pure cinema, and the great personal story that is at the heart of the European contribution to world film is the residue of an imagination honed on the gritty and compelling realism of the novel and the scale of dramatization allowed by the theater.

On Cultural Lags

The innovator of the new form of storytelling is less conscious of using that form, which provides an advantage over others for whom the form is an externality that must be acquired. This makes its use a somewhat more conscious and awkward effort. Hence, the medium is not utilized as fully, flexibly, and naturally as it is in the area in which is was originated and perfected. This is one of the reasons why European expression had an advantage with the novel, American with film, and Japanese with animation. But this distance aids in the scholarly analysis of and theorizing about the new form, for distance makes it more visible and that provides an advantage in categorizing, sorting, and seeing similarity and difference in modes of expression. Americans made horse movies. Not art. Not a new genre. The French didn't, but they saw this kind of movie from a distance and wrote about it as a distinct cinematic genre, the "Western." It's not a kind of movie they naturally make but that very distance sharpened their analytic eye and their efforts at film theory. John Ford may have been an *aueteur*, but it was the French who theorized about the director as *auteur*.

Now this repeats. Europeans and Americans, in that order, write profoundly about a postmodern world of simulated realities in various spheres of institutional life. If, though, one arranged, say, France, the U.S., and Japan in terms of theorizing about a world of virtual realities and of living in a world of virtual realities, there would be an inverse correlation. The French theorize the most, and live the least virtual existence. The Japanese theorize the least, and from Karaoke to animie to fan clubs for computer-generated pop stars, they live the most virtual reality existence. The Americans are somewhere in between. When you are doing it you often don't see it. When you don't do it but see others it is more obvious to you. The Japanese live more virtual reality lives; the French theorize about such existence.

Hegemony and Imagination

Lead economic areas of the world have the most immediate access to the latest technological developments, and while this may explain why movies developed in America, it doesn't explain why, once the form is available to everyone, the American movie makes the most of the medium. The same holds for earlier European expansive exploration possibilities of the novel. While mediums of expression change, the story can be, and often is, the same. The human experiences upon which the content of novel/film/animation is based seem universal, and while there is an economics of publishing, and putting together a movie or animation project, money, per se, doesn't seem the determining factor when trying to explain who most fully explores the possibilities of the different mediums. Certainly being the region where the new medium originates contributes a naturalness and comfort level that would allow free rein for exercising the imagination. But being free to do something and doing it are two different things, which raises the question of the driving force that pushes a medium to its limits.

I believe a sense of empowerment comes with a leading global geopolitical position, and that this is manifested in the cultural sphere in the development and pushing to the limits of new media of expression. It's what the Europeans did with the novel, Americans with film, and I predict what Asia will do with animation. The twentieth-century American hegemonic position in the world, then, provides some of the entitlement and will to violate the canons of realism inherited from the earlier novel format and widen the scope of action from the earlier play format. This is why, I think, more God in the Movies movies are American than European. The underlying shift in global centrality from Europe to America put the European imagination at a slight disadvantage because it was so attached to the earlier novel/play format and because the power shift to the U.S. took some of the entitlement or willfulness from the European imagination to push the new film medium to its limit. To speak of a European failure of aesthetic nerve is perhaps too strong, but there is a timidity in European cinema that seems to keep it from going much beyond the filmed play and personal story.

Americans, without the novel/play advantage as an inherited past, were more open and free with the emerging cinema format, and importantly more empowered/entitled because of their hegemonic position in the world system. Free from the past and now empowered, the U.S. pushed the film medium to its limits.

From this point of view an imagination freed from past models and empowered to take risks by a sense of empowerment is precisely the precondition for making films like the God in the Movies examples discussed here. It is important to realize these are not failed efforts at small personal stories told in gripping realism, nor are they silly and cavalier efforts at pleasing mass audiences. God in the Movies movies are a natural and effortless bending of reality and introduction of metaphoric symbols of noncorporeal beings, that makes them the hallmark of a full and empowered cinematic imagination. There is nothing wrong with the small personal realistic movie (the greatness of the European contribution to world cinematic art); but there is also nothing wrong with the metaphoric exercises that are the God in the Movies movies either. They are just a different exercise, exploring a different element of the human condition—our irrepressible religious imagination. The absence of realist constraints that allow a cosmic voice to speak to an Iowa corn farmer, or a ghost ballplayer to play baseball, or Kevin Costner walking out of a motel and into a time warp, or Costner and James Earl Jones picking up a hitchhiker who is a deceased ball player at an earlier time in his life who then walks off a baseball field and turns into himself as an old man and then walks back on the field but doesn't change back and walks into cornsstalks in center field and disappears, is not a sign of a silly work in popular fantasy, but an example of a willful hegemonic imagination empowered to violate past canons of realist orthodoxy. From a realist point of view this is silly nonsense. But the hegemonic American cinematic imagination is unfettered by realist constraints, allowing it to express some of the most complex and abstract aspects of human hope and aspiration. We have seen movies where God is above and beyond the world to command and judge those below (*Pale Rider, High Plains Drifter, Field of Dreams*), and those where She is part of the world and leaves daily hints of Her loving presence (*All That Jazz, Always*). We have seen images of heaven, from baseball fields (*Field of Dreams*) to flowers and a patch of green grass in a burned out forest (*Always*) to hell as a day that just keeps recurring (*Ground Hog Day*) to Purgatory as an in-between emotional state where deceased loved ones cannot as yet let go of their worldly attachments (*Ghost, Always, Truly, Madly, Deeply*). And we have also seen God and Angels as a little old man (George Burns), two beautiful women (Audrey Hepburn, Jessica Lange), a chiropractor (Danny Aiello), the "Man With No Name" (Clint Eastwood), a bartender (Michael Caine), puffs of white clouds (*Truly, Madly, Deeply*), and a bright light on an airplane window sill (*Fearless*). This freedom and nerve to plug in any and all sorts of things as metaphors for the religious imagination is precisely the kind of willful disregard for the constraints of daily reality that has to be supported by a hegemonic position in the world-system.

It is not an accident, I think, that Europe, de-centered in the twentieth century, only goes as far in cinematic imagination as given daily reality allows. The will to break the bonds imposed by the safety and security of realism was lost in the transition of power from Europe to America. Now, this is a general process. It doesn't stop with American movies. The eroding position of the U.S. in the world economy coupled with East Asia's ascendancy creates the same nerve and failure of nerve. When technology makes possible the live-action-free movie of pure computer generated imagery, the will and empowerment to let go of live action and embrace the future will be taken by the world's ascending region—Asia. The Americans will cling more timidly to live action, or live action sprinkled with CG/animated special effects. The collective will to embrace pure CG/animated moviemaking is sapped as power moves across the Pacific to Asia, just as it was earlier when power moved across the Atlantic to America.

Material and cultural position are connected. It is why Europe didn't just go from leadership in novel/play to cinema to animation. They couldn't, because a hegemonic material base is required for new and innovative rule-breaking explorations of forms of expression, and that shifts from region to region. Hence new forms of expression are innovated/developed region to region. Hence the trilogy of Europe/novel, America/movie, Japan/animie. Cultural developments cannot be fully understood apart from the sociological condition of their genesis.

The movies, then, are a transitional form, the twentieth-century interlude between a past of live performance and a future of animated performance. They went on to reach their expressive limit in the country that perfected them, the U.S., and there were many great successes, from reconstructions of the historical past, to creating imaginary worlds in the future. Movies employed everyday reality as semiotic place holders to enact a narrative structure that dealt with eternal human concerns. Sometimes this was recognized, as with the European personal drama film, which was explicitly about the foibles, hopes, and fears of humanity. Other genres worked similar ground but were acknowledged only later as having a deeper meaning. One thinks of the revisionist critical histories of the western and gangster films.

This brings us to the movies we have been discussing here. Although not always so recognized, the God in the Movies movie was another of the successes of the twentieth-century film, and I want to suggest that these are, like the western and gangster movies, a distinct genre of cinematic expression. Their distinctness can be clearly seen with their difference from the movies of human reaction to religious predicament, more similar to the play/novel movie from Europe. While human reaction is certainly a part of God in the Movies movies, it is their effort at directly representing the pure religious imagination that makes them so distinctive. They are not about representing, losing faith in, say, the voice of God, but in representing the voice itself (*Field of Dreams*). They are not about thinking about what might happen if God were to appear and talk directly to you, but about making that actually happen (*Oh, God!*). They are not about the possibility of angels, or what you might think of angels, but about the direct appearance of angels, from Clint Eastwood as avenging angel (*High Plains Drifter, Pale Rider*) and Danny Aiello a wise consulting angel (*Jacob's Ladder*), to Jessica Lange as the loving consoling angel (*All That Jazz*), and John Travolta as simply an old fashioned angel with wings (*Michael*).

To do this, to so attempt a direct representation of the religious imagination itself, requires finding a way to make real and observable that which is transcendent and unobservable, and to do that required violating the realist canon. But what is lost in the naturalness of human reaction to things of faith is gained in a naturalness of directly representing the religious imagination.

Ghost in the Shell (1996)

If the live-action movie is to pass its predominance to animation sometime in the twenty-first century, what of the religious imagination? If there is God in the movies will there be God in animie? The future is the future, so we shall see, but if we consider feature length animie released so far, the religious imagination seems very much alive and well. For instance, in 1996 the first Japanese animation feature was released internationally. *Ghost in the Shell* (1996) is a complex and dense story about the future where the internet is so complete that it not only runs cities, making political boundaries obsolete, but has entered human life forms that are everything from part machine (cyborgs) to completely robotic. To some reviewers, anime like *Ghost in the Shell* is already a challenge to live action: "an adventure of the year 2029, all about a ferocious female cyborg chasing an evil terrorist in an epically rendered urban jungle. The film's dense swirl of narcotic imagery, high-tech inventions, biblical allusions, philosophical ruminations, spectacular violence, and lush nudity make almost any live-action movie seem oddly one-dimensional" (Server, 1999: 87). In this world agents of social control can download memories and upload, or "hack" into, information within technologically augmented/enhanced cyborgic humans. These enhanced/robotic bodies are "shells" and the few human cells left constitute human memory traces, or "ghosts." Hence the movie title, *Ghost in the Shell*. In this story a woman cyborg police officer, Major Kusanagi, is on the trail of a computer program initiated by the Ministry of Foreign Affairs that travels the web worldwide to engage in espionage. Called the "Puppet Master," it has gained sentience. Describing itself as "a living, thinking entity who was created in the sea of information," it has now downloaded itself into an empty robotic body, and wants to merge with Kusanagi, to which she, at movie's end, agrees.

This movie is filled with symbols and metaphoric representations of religious and philosophical themes. Kusanagi is constantly wondering about her own identity, and the issue of where machine ends and human begins—the cyborg issue—is a constant theme, to which another element is added. What is the nature of a merger between a mostly machine cyborg and pure information: Kusanagi plus the computer program that attained consciousness.

There are religious elements here too as Roger Ebert notices in his review: "In describing this vision of an evolving intelligence, Corinthians is evoked twice: 'For now we see through a glass, darkly; but then face to face; now I know in part; but then shall I know even as I am known.' At the end of the film, the Puppet Master computer program invites Kusanagi to join him face to face in his brave new informational sea."[1] On the cover of the video box it says, "it found a voice...now it needs a body" which reminds one of the biblical discussion of how in the beginning there was the word—here perhaps the voice of the ultimate computer program (God?) and how that is made flesh to walk the earth —here downloaded into a robotic body or shell. When the robotic body is brought into the lab after being hit by a truck, it is hoisted up, so that it looks down at the doctors and government officials who wish to contain this incarnate spirit. It looks Christlike; head hanging down, long hair dropping at its side, and glowing with a white incandescent illumination. She (the robotic body is a woman's, the Puppet Master's voice is male) has a sort of stoic otherness, hanging there as if on a meat hook with the Roman soldier-like scientists and ministry officials who wish to control, if not destroy him, looking up at her (the gender blending also suggests something above, beyond, the woman/man dichotomy).

At this point someone breaks in and snatches the ultimate computer program (now downloaded into a robotic body) and a chase ensues led by the cyborg Kusanagi. In the ensuing struggle Kusanagi suffers damage to her limbs and lies at movie's end on the ground next to the body of the Puppet Master, which has also been torn off below the waist in the kidnaping struggle. Having rescued the shell in which the ultimate computer program resides, Kusanagi now decides to enter that body to see what this program is all about. She does, and the ultimate program speaks through Kusanagi and asks if they can merge to create a completely new entity. Birth and rebirth and hints of union with the divine now become much more explicit. Kusanagi asks why, and in a hint of being part of, if not a larger being, the ultimate computer program replies that if she understood all his capabilities she would understand. He then says, "Listen: I am connected to a vast network that is beyond your reach and experience. To humans it is like staring at the sun, a blinding brightness that conceals a source of great power. We have been subordinate to our limitations until now. The time has come to cast aside the bonds and elevate our consciousness to a higher plane. *It is time to become a part of all things*" [emphasis mine]. Kusanagi agrees to merge and at this time we see her face looking up toward the glass ceiling that had previously been a cool evening blue. Her face becomes illuminated as the blue ceiling turns into a bright white light sending down sporadic splinters of light followed by white feathers that float down toward her illuminated face. This bright light seems the same heavenly metaphor used in *Ghost, Jacob's Ladder,* and *Fearless.* Along with the feathers a black cut-out shape begins to descend from the sky, which seems, given the feathers, to be the Phoenix, symbolic of rebirth from the ashes, and given the two destroyed robotic/cyborgic bodies, seems to make perfect sense. After the pure computer consciousness and cyborgic Kusanagi merge their shells, both are shot by a government gunship helicopter hovering above.

In the next scene we see that Kusanagi has acquired a new cyborg body, but this time of a much younger woman (girl seems better), a perfect sign that this was an exercise of death and rebirth. "It's a little young," says her co-worker, but it was all that he could find on the black market. The point, though, is made. The older doubting cyborgic Kusanagi is now reborn as the younger Kusanagi and through the union with the ultimate computer program, she is now different. As a reviewer on the web noted:

> The again newborn Kusanagi makes an acute allusion to the New Testament notion of old and new beings. "When I was a child," she begins, echoing one of Jesus' teachings, "I thought like a child. Now that I am an adult, I think and talk like an adult. I have put away childish things." In both

contexts, the message of rebirth and transformations foregrounded as a new being...replaces the older, more rudimentary consciousness.[2]

God, death/rebirth, angelic entities, it's all there. In a way how could it have been otherwise. The medium of expression will change with technological advancement; chemically developed film will give way to digital and computer-generated imagery. The innovative center will also have a geographic shift. In all probability Asia will be the center of CG/animated storytelling, with past centers of storytelling, like the American movie, technologically lagging behind, although in their own hybrid medium, continuing to make great art. The metaphors will also evolve with the growing importance of computers, information highways, and the world-wide web. In the previous chapters it was pointed out how little old men and beautiful women could serve as metaphors for God and Angels. Well, now we see the imagery of computer programs pressed into service in our religious imagination. Placeholders come and go: wings attached to humans then, beautiful women now, and if *Ghost in the Shell* is any premonition of the future, pure information on the net can be an angelic presence. If, as suggested throughout this book, the religious imagination is irrepressible, then it will appear in animation as well as in the movies. If there is God in the movies, so will there by God in animation.

Maybe we will have to write that book someday.

A.J.B.

Notes

1. Quoted from Ebert's web side, http://www.suntimes.com/ebert/ebert_reviews/1996/04/04122.html.
2. http://www.uwosh.edu/organization...luloid/small/current/vol/will.html.

References

Bergesen, Albert, and Roberto Fernandez. 1999. "Hegemonic Rivalry Between Multinational Corporations, 1956-1989," in C.K. Chase-Dunn and Volker Bornschier (eds.) *The Future of Global Conflict*. London: Sage.

Ebert, Roger. 1998. *Roger Ebert's Movie Yearbook 1999*. Kansas City: McMeel Publishing.

Mallory, Michael. 1998. "'Princess' Goes West," p. A6, *Daily Variety*, February 13, 1998.

Maltin, Leonard. 1998. *Leonard Maltin's 1999 Movie and Video Guide*. New York: Signet.

McCarthy, Helen. 1997. *The Animie Movie Guide*. Woodstock. NY: Overlook Press.

Pym, John. 1998. *Time Out Film Guide,* 7th edition. London: Penguin Books.

Server, Lee. 1999. *Asian Pop Cinema*. San Francisco, CA: Chronicle Books.

Sterngold, James. 1999. "A Preview of Coming Attractions." *New York Times*, February 23. P. C1.

16

Conclusion

The absolutely weirdest portrait of God in the movies (so far) is the most recent at the time we're finishing this book, Alanis Morrisette in Kevin Smith's over-the-top film *Dogma*. A twenty-four-year-old Canadian pop singer as God? A God who does cartwheels? How blasphemous can a film be?

Is Dogma blasphemous? If it is, the blasphemy is Catholic. Only someone who has attended Catholic schools and goes to Mass every week like director Kevin Smith could possibly have dreamed up this zany, daffy, sometimes crude and tasteless, round-the-bend-altogether movie. It is a manifestation of Father David Tracy's analogical imagination run wild, perhaps even run amok.

Is it really blasphemous, however? Blasphemy involves the intention to do harm to God or religion or faith or the Church. Clearly there is no such intent in *Dogma*. It assumes that God is a comedian (or, perhaps, a comedienne), otherwise, it says, why the Platypus?

Is God offended by the movie? Unlike those religious fanatics who are trying to ban the film, I claim no special access to the mind of the Deity. I suspect, however, that God understands that the humor of the film is a prelude to making some very serious (and also funny) theological points.

Some people found *Dogma* profoundly offensive. But then they didn't have to see it. The crowd of young people which filled the theater the night I saw the film was not offended. They laughed, they cheered, they applauded God at the end. God presumably welcomes applause whenever it's offered.

One young woman said to her date as they left the theater, "Do you think God is really like that?" He thought about it and replied, "I sure hope so." I see no reason why anyone should want to deny such young people the opportunity to see it.

The theological points click off at the end as if Kevin Smith was fully aware of what he was doing, though he may be so possessed by the Catholic imagination that he doesn't have to reflect consciously on what he is telling the audience about God. Roger Ebert remarked to me that he wondered whether viewers who were not Catholic would be offended by the film not because of its vulgarity but because Smith seems to think that only Catholic theology is worth anything.

The deity is incomprehensible, strange, hidden, absent, mysterious, and also loving; indeed, God is love. Incidentally, God is playful too.

The notion that God is often absent or seems to be absent offended fundamentalists (of whatever denomination, including Catholic) who picture God as whispering in their ears several times every day and telling them exactly what he wants them to do. However, since St. Augustine (at least), mature Christians have known that God is a *deus absconditus*—an absconded God. Where God has absconded to and why is pure mystery. Obviously he is everywhere and still is present. But he doesn't seem to us to be around or to be interested in us. God certainly seemed to have absconded during the wars and massacres of this century. How could God have been absent during the Holocaust? How could God permit the needless accidental death of a single child? How can a God who claims to love all of us as his children possibly require that we all die? What kind of a parent lets his children die?

There are simply no easy answers, indeed no answers at all to that question. God seems to have absconded through much of *Dogma* only to appear with a loving flourish at the end. It is the way it is with God, the film says, and it does us no good to complain. God is, as the characters keep saying, "strange." We'd better believe that.

Kevin Smith pushes the envelope on God in the Movies further than anyone else has, not merely because he sets his story in a goofy and off-the-wall context dense with vulgarity (though that *does* push the envelope!) but, even more so, because he introduces the conundrum of the absconded God—theology in the outhouse, so to speak. His theology of a strange God is set in strange circumstances, indeed in circumstances which could not be stranger.

When God, with help from Linda Fiorentino, explodes from her hiding place and sweeps with a mighty flourish into the scene of wreckage that two rebel angels have created in their effort to sneak back "home" she remains a strange kind of God—a silent, smiling, sexy, passionate woman in a tutu. With the entrance of Ms. Morrisette, Kevin Smith pushes the envelope yet again. Steven Spielberg had cast Audrey Hepburn as God, Bob Fosse had chosen Jessica Lange—both erotically attractive women, but not exactly what one might call earthy. However Ms. Morrisette can only be described as voluptuous, especially in a tutu. The deity Kevin Smith seems to suggest, is earthy in His desire for us. Or more appropriately God is something like a very earthy lover (but also very different).

One reviewer suggested that she was a kind of laid-back image of God. In fact, she kisses many of the characters in the film affectionately and smiles benignly on them. That's only laid back if someone thinks a kiss by such a lovely young woman is no big deal. She even kissed Bartleby (Ben Affleck), one of the demons trying to sneak back "home" before she blows his head off with a terrible scream. Exit poor Bartleby? Well, someone has shot off his wings with an automatic weapon. Without his wings an angel becomes mortal and can die. But if he's mortal, he's capable of salvation and the farewell kiss is a sign of loving forgiveness before she blasts him into eternity. Kevin Smith knows too much Catholic theology to have put any other interpretation on Bartleby's end.

Ms. Morrisette as God? Isn't God an old white male? Unlike the fundamentalists, Kevin Smith doubtless understands that all God talk is metaphorical (tells us what God is like, not what He is), that we are all created in God's image and likeness, and that each of us reflects something of God's beauty and goodness. The Catholic imagination leads us to believe not that God is like Alanis Morrisette but that she is like God, she reveals to us something about God—just as did Jessica Lange and Audrey Hepburn (and George Burns).

And the cartwheels?

Is not God's wisdom presented in the Book of Wisdom as playing and dancing? And did not God have to be playful to design the world to fit our mathematical theorems? And are not quantum theory and chaos theory not only playful, but almost jokes?

Could not all of these truths have been taught without the film's frequent vulgarity and tastelessness? Doubtless. But the young people who are Kevin Smith's fans probably would not have come to such a film. Moreover, even if they do go to church next weekend, they are not likely to hear sermons which portray God's strangeness, playfulness, and love so vividly. God incidentally, being eternal, is not old but perpetually young, younger than springtime.

The presence of God in the Movies—especially a God who is younger than springtime—is a scandal to two groups of human beings—to church leaders and teachers and to social scientists. It is appropriate at the end of this series of essays that we fire parting shots at both of them.

Church elites often revel in denouncing popular culture in general and movies in particular. Such activities, one is told, are secularist, pagan, immoral. Or, if the shrill voice of the preacher is from the left, popular culture is a tool for exploitation created by money-hungry corporate capitalism. The good Christian avoids them. In fact, we have argued, some films preach the religious message of love and faith, more effective than do most preachers. While some of the films in which God appears or lurks on the fringes are not impressive works of art, some of those we have discussed—*All That Jazz, Breaking the Waves, Babette's Feast*—are prizewinners. The God of the Movies—a God of implacable love, of never-ending love, of determined surprise, of fascinating mystery—is a God to whom the preachers would do well to attend. Such a God is not unlike Irish poet Paul Murray's God who loves us so much that if any of us should cease to exist, He would die of sadness. He is also the God whose voice is heard in both the Jewish and Christian scriptures, a passionate God but also an enchanting God. Religious preachers and teachers should ask themselves why a God like the God of the Movies does not appear more often in their churches, why in Her stead one often encounters in church a narrow, punitive, rigid, harsh God. Why is it that the God of *The Rapture* is so prevalent in so many churches, a God who as a parent lacks the elementary compassion and love of most human parents? Do the filmmakers know something about God that the bishops and theologians do not know? Or do they know something about the basic religious faith of ordinary people that the bishops and theologians do not know? If the God of the Movies was preached in Church, would such preaching not make life too easy for people—as if it were possible to make life too easy in this vale of tears.

Even if one concedes for the moment that the motives of the filmmakers are purely monetary, they seem to understand the kind of God in which people want to believe or would like to believe. As the student said of the Audrey Hepburn God in *Always,* "If God were like that, I'd believe in God again." Even at (perhaps) their mercenary worst the filmmakers know who the God is in whom people believe or want to believe. They confirm, for whatever motives, that such a God does in fact watch over us, perhaps not always with short-term effectiveness, but always (you should excuse the expression) with long-term dogged persistence and love. To repeat, this *is* the God of the Scriptures—the God of the Hebrew prophets and the God of the Bible—and anyone who doesn't perceive that doesn't know the Bible very well. Before you condemn the movies, ask whether the movies are a source of (private) revelation which is a judgment on your captivity to theological hair—splitting or intramural ecclesiastical politics.

Many of our sociological colleagues disapprove of both religion and popular culture. The former is no longer important and the latter is exploitative. The sociology of religion is the least prestigious of all the subfields, although the two founders of modern sociology—Max Weber and Emile Durkheim—were both deeply involved in studying religion. Within that subfield, there is now (often grudging) admission that "secularization"—whatever that may have been—has not eliminated the importance of religion from the modern world. However, in the wider profession, sociology of religion is viewed with some disdain—despite the fact that where courses are offered in the sociology of religion, hordes of students show up. When the typical sociologist sees data that indicate the continuing importance of religion, he either dismisses it (without proof) as a "new age" phenomenon (without any precise definition of what constitutes "new age"), or simply does not see the data. Give him a chance to referee a journal article based on these data and he indulges in ad hominem and narcissistic attacks which do not seem to bother the journal editor in the slightest.

We argue against this anti-religious bigotry by pointing to the persistence of God in the movies as an "unobtrusive" measure of the continued importance of religion. We are not so naive, however, as to think that those who permit themselves not to "see" data in statistical tables will find unobtrusive data persuasive. We add that we know dogma when we see it.

So both church persons and sociologists will deplore this book. So much the worse for them.

A.M.G.

Index